Taking Liberties

Tomarse Libertades

by Felipe Galindo Feggo

The book *Taking Liberties* was made possible in part with public funds from
Creative Engagement, supported by the New York City Department of Cultural Affairs
in partnership with the City Council, administered by
the Lower Manhattan Cultural Council.
LMCC serves, connects and makes space for artists and community.

For more on the work of Felipe Galindo,
please visit feggo.com

Edited & Designed by Martin Kozlowski
please visit martinkozlowski.com

For more on Now What Media Books,
please visit nowwhatmedia.com/nowwhatbooks.html

This book may be purchased in bulk for promotional, educational or business purposes.
Please contact editor @ nowwhatmedia.com

Introduction

From the day it was dedicated on October 28, 1886, the Statue of Liberty has embodied the best values of my adopted country, and the ideals for which she stands — like the abolition of slavery, as well as liberty, democracy, freedom, the American Dream, human rights, peace and opportunity — make her a beacon of hope for many.

Learning of the statue's deep significance for the American people left an impact on me and inspired me to read the history of French artist Bartholdi's project, and I was amazed to discover everything that Lady Liberty represents.

My first encounter with the Statue of Liberty was as a tourist, back in 1981, a different experience than that of the Statue welcoming European immigrants at the New York City harbor. Lady Liberty is an iconic image that has been used in innumerable ways and depicted in art, films, cartoons — political or not — and in all types of merchandise, like souvenirs, T-shirts, postcards, statues, and costumes.

As a cartoon and illustration artist, I have depicted her in many contexts, from everyday life situations to imagining her taking political stances. "Taking Liberties" is a collection of images I've been creating since I moved to New York City from my native Mexico in 1983. It is an homage, from the perspective of an immigrant artist, of a symbol that speaks to all of us. With this project, I continue my exploration of the intersections of art, history, and humor in my work.

The project addresses identity, equality, and justice, issues so relevant in the current socio-political climate in the US and the world. During the Trump administration (1/20/2017 – 1/20/2021), Lady Liberty was for me — and I think for many — a symbol of resistance against the policies that in many instances went against the norms of democracy and the values of this country.

Fortunately the outcome of the most recent election turned the tide towards a more positive course. I do hope the country continues to make progress to achieve social justice for all.

Felipe Galindo Feggo

Introducción

Desde el día en que se inauguró, el 28 de octubre de 1886, la Estatua de la Libertad ha representado los mejores valores de mi país adoptivo, y los ideales que simboliza — la abolición de la esclavitud, la democracia, la libertad, el sueño Americano, los derechos humanos, la paz, y la oportunidad — la han hecho un emblema de esperanza para muchos.

El querer conocer el profundo significado de este símbolo del pueblo estadounidense me inspiró a leer la historia del proyecto del artista francés Bartholdi, y fue entonces que descubrí todo lo que representa la Dama Libertad.

Mi primer encuentro con ella fue como turista en 1981, una experiencia muy diferente de aquella noción romántica de los inmigrantes europeos que llegaban en barco y a quienes les daba la bienvenida al puerto de la ciudad de Nueva York. La Estatua de la Libertad es una imágen icónica y ha sido utilizada en arte, películas, caricaturas — políticas y no — y en mercancía como souvenirs turísticos, camisetas, postales, reproducciones, disfraces, etc.

En mi trabajo como dibujante de humor y artista visual, ella me he inspirado a plasmarla en muchas ocasiones, desde en situaciones de vida cotidiana hasta imaginándola tomando posiciones políticas. "Taking Liberties/ Tomarse Libertades" es una colección de imágenes que he realizado desde mi arribo a la ciudad de New York en 1983 cuando emigré de mi México natal. El proyecto es un homenaje desde el punto de vista de un artista inmigrante, a un símbolo tan importante para todos. Con este proyecto, continúo mi exploración de las intersecciones del arte, la historia el humor.

El proyecto aborda temas de identidad, equidad y justicia, tan relevantes en el actual clima sociopolítico en Estados Unidos y el mundo entero. Durante la administración Trump (1/20/2017 – 1/20/2021) la Dama Libertad fue para mí — y creo que para muchos — un símbolo de resistencia a las políticas que en muchos casos iban en contra de las normas de la democracia y el espíritu de este país.

Afortunadamente, el resultado de la más reciente elección nos enfila hacia un rumbo más positivo. Espero que el país siga progresando hacia una sociedad que logre la justicia social para todos.

Felipe Galindo Feggo

The Statue of Liberty:
A Brief History

The Statue of Liberty was a gift of friendship from France to the U.S. for the centennial of its independence. A symbol of freedom and democracy designed and built by sculptor Frederic Auguste Bartholdi, the impressive monument stands at 151 feet (46 meters) high, and at 305 (93 meters) including the pedestal.

It was fabricated with 60,000 pounds of copper with a 250,000 pound steel inner structure, designed by Gustave Eiffel.

When he created the sculpture, which represents the Roman goddess *Libertas* (equivalent of the Greek goddess *Eleutheria*,) Bartholdi was inspired by several important historical works of art, like the Colossus of Rhodes, one of the Seven Wonders of the Ancient World. It would have been interesting to see the statue in her original reddish brown copper color, as opposed to the current oxidized green.

The work took fifteen years to complete, from a visit Bartholdi made to New York in June of 1871, until it was dedicated on October 28, 1886. He was also inspired by ideas from French writer, professor, and politician Edouard René de Labouyale. He considered the United States a modern example of a republic, having written a three-volume book about its history. He also proposed a united effort to build a monument in America as a memorial to both countries' friendship, independence, and freedom following the Union's victory after the Civil War.

The French financed the sculpture, on the condition that the U.S. finance the pedestal and secure a site for the work. After the sculpture was completed in France, the piece was shipped in 350 sections, inside more than 200 cases. The US selected Bedloe island in the New York City harbor and changed its name to Liberty Island.

The statue's official name is "Liberty Enlightening the World"; the torch and seven spikes — like rays of light — on her crown are meant to symbolize that.

The tablet in her left hand, a *tabula ansata*, has dovetail handles as in the design of Imperial Rome and bears the inscription "July 4, 1776," date of the Declaration of Independence. The broken chains at her feet commemorate the then-recent abolition of slavery.

Lady Liberty would later become associated with immigration, as newcomers stood in awe as their ships approached Ellis Island, the busiest inspection station in the country.

The poem by Emma Lazarus "The New Colossus," written for an art and literary works auction to raise money for Lady Liberty's pedestal, emphasizes this association. The poem was later cast on a bronze plaque and placed inside the pedestal. The poem evokes a welcome ode for immigrants, still relevant today:

"Give me your tired, your poor,

Your huddled masses yearning to breathe free,

The wretched refuse of your teeming shore.

Send these, the homeless, tempest-tost to me,

I lift my lamp beside the golden door!"

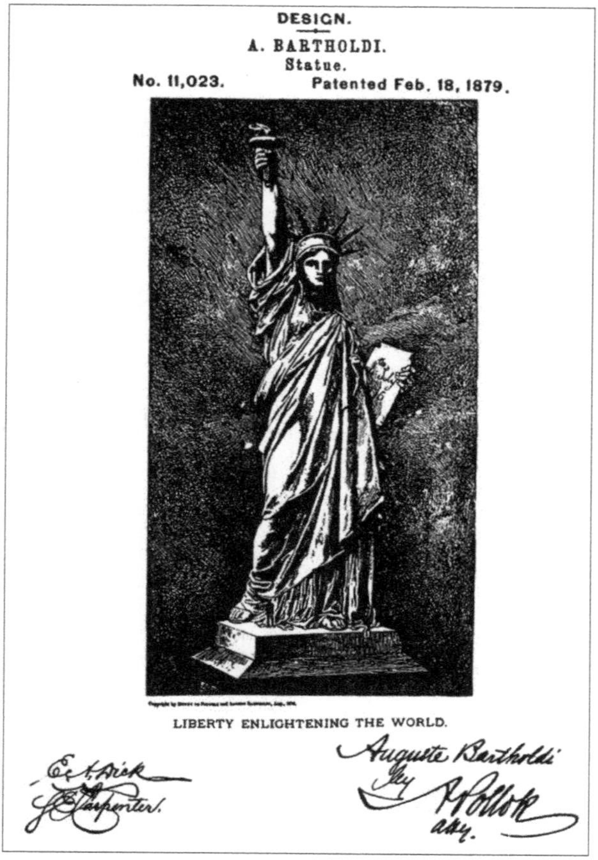
DESIGN.
A. BARTHOLDI.
Statue.
No. 11,023.
Patented Feb. 18, 1879.
LIBERTY ENLIGHTENING THE WORLD.

La Estatua De La Libertad: Una Breve Historia

La Estatua fue un regalo de Amistad de Francia a los Estados Unidos por el centenario de su independencia. Un símbolo de libertad y democracia diseñado y construído por el escultor Frederic Auguste Bartholdi con 30 toneladas de cobre y con una estructura interior de 125 toneladas de acero. Es un monumento impresionante por sus 46 metros de altura o 93 metros incluyendo el pedestal.

Bartholdi se inspiró en históricas obras de arte — como el Coloso de Rodas, una de las 7 maravillas del mundo antiguo — cuando creó su escultura, quien representa a la diosa romana Libertas (equivalente a la diosa griega Eleuteria). Sería interesante haber visto la escultura en su color original de cobre, un marrón rojizo, antes de oxidarse al verde actual.

Tomó a Bartholdi 15 años en completar su proyecto, desde su visita inicial a Nueva York en junio de 1871 hasta que se inauguró el 28 de octubre de 1886. Bartholdi se inspiró también en las ideas del escritor, profesor y político francés Edouard René de Labouyale, quien consideraba a los Estados Unidos como un gran ejemplo de república moderna. El había escrito 3 volúmenes sobre su historia y propuso un esfuerzo conjunto para construir en los Estados Unidos un monumento a la amistad de ambos países, a la independencia y la libertad tras la victoria de la Unión en la Guerra Civil.

Los franceses financiaron la estatua con la condición de que los Estados Unidos finaciaran el pedestal y designaran un lugar donde instalarla. Una vez que el proyecto se completó en Francia, se envió en 350 partes en más de 200 cajas. Se asignó la isla Bedloe en el puerto de la ciudad de Nueva York para su instalación y cambió su nombre a Liberty Island o Isla de la Libertad.

Su nombre oficial es "Libertad que ilumina el mundo" y la antorcha y los siete picos como rayos de luz en su cabeza lo simbolizan. La "tabula ansata" en su mano izquierda — tablilla con asas de cola de paloma, diseño de la Roma Imperial — tiene la fecha 4 de Julio de 1776, día de la Declaración de Independencia, en números romanos. Las cadenas a sus pies conmemoran la entonces reciente abolición de la esclavitud.

A la Dama Libertad se le asociaría después con la inmigración, ya que los barcos llenos de recién llegados pasaban junto a ella rumbo a Ellis Island donde eran registrados al arribo a su nuevo país. También aumentó esta asociación el poema "El Nuevo Coloso" — ahora muy famoso — de Emma Lazarus, escrito para una subasta de obras literarias y de arte y cuyo objetivo era recaudar dinero para el pedestal de la estatua. Posteriormente el poema se reprodujo en una placa de bronce y se colocó dentro de dicho pedestal.

La segunda parte del poema evoca una oda de bienvenida a los inmigrantes, y es muy relevante estos días, como a continuación leeremos:

"Denme a sus cansados, a sus pobres,

a sus masas que anhelan respirar libremente.

Envíen a sus desamparados, arrojados por la tormenta.

¡Alzo mi antorcha junto a la puerta dorada!

Taking Liberties

Tomarse Libertades

**Lady Liberty Before
the November 2016 Elections**

La Dama Libertad Antes
de las Elecciones de Noviembre del 2016

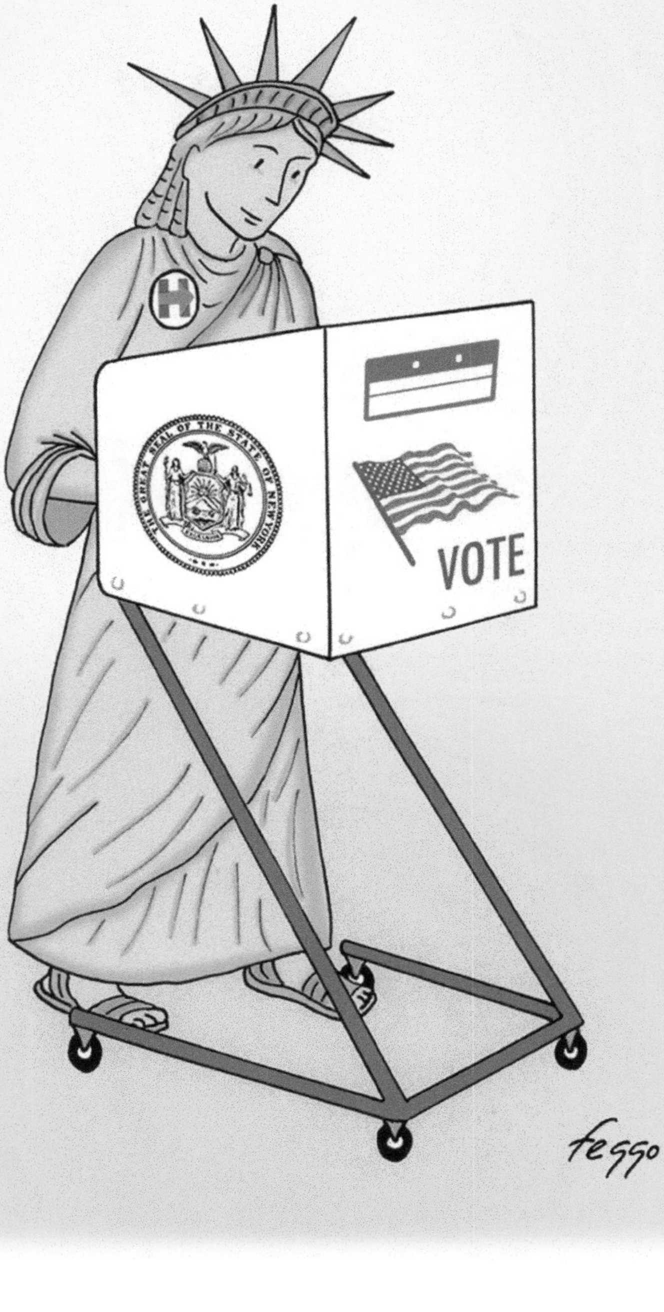
THE GREAT SEAL OF THE STATE OF NEW YORK
VOTE
feggo

Lady Liberty After the 2016 Elections

I previously used this image to reflect on the 9/11/2001 terrorist attacks. I found the sentiment of millions was similar after the results of the 2016 elections and also after the domestic terrorist attack to the Nation's Capitol on 1/6/2021. Inspired by the painting "Old Man in Sorrow" by Vincent Van Gogh.

La Dama Libertad Después de las Elecciones del 2016

Esta imágen la utilicé anteriormente para reflejar el sentimiento de la nación tras los ataques terroristas del 11 de septiembre en 2001, sentimientos similares para millones tras las elecciones del 2016 y también tras el ataque terrorista doméstico al Capitolio, el 6 de enero de 2021.

Inspirado en la pintura "Hombre Viejo Afligido" de Vicente Van Gogh.

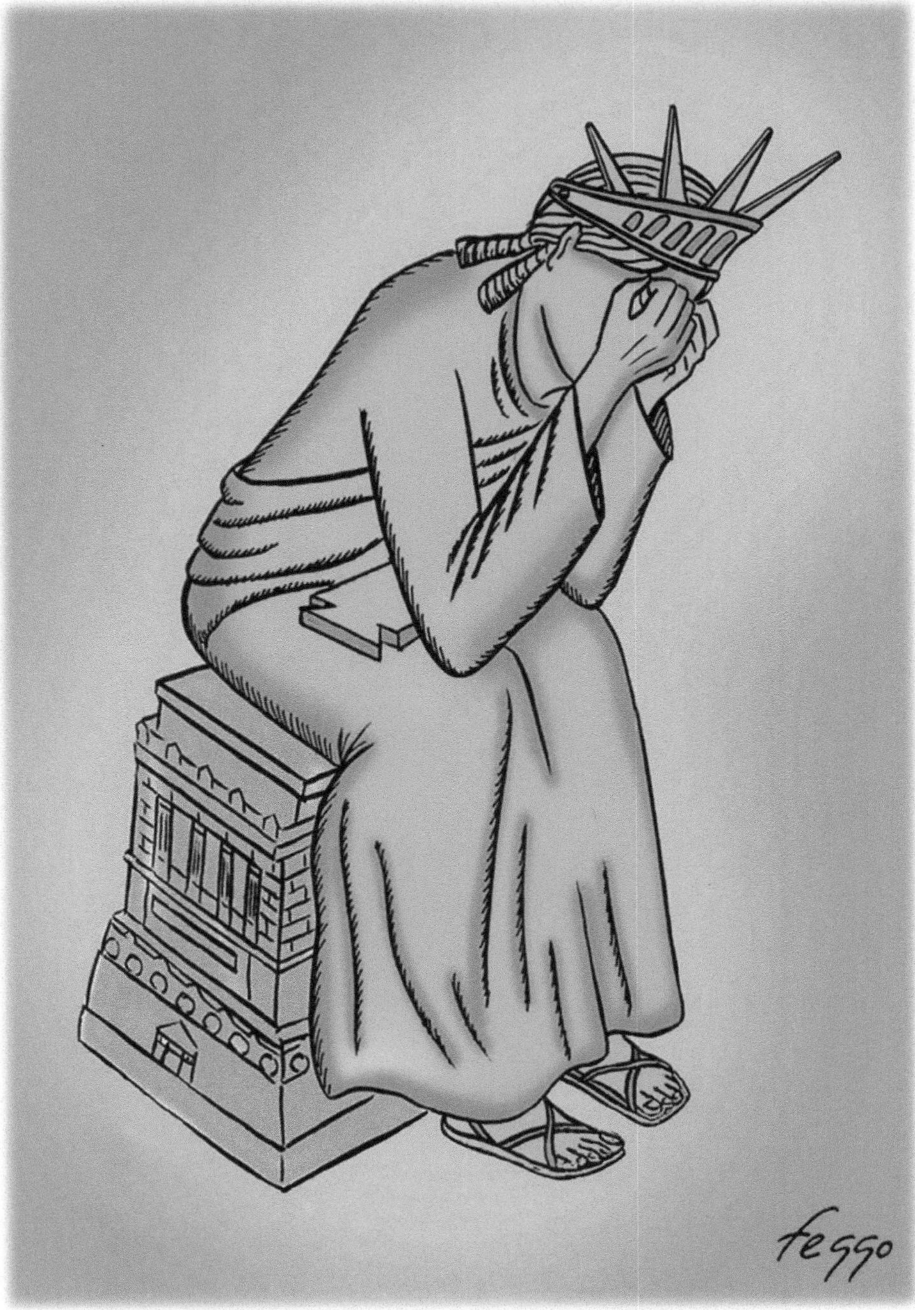
feggo

Lady Liberty Calling to Resist

La Dama Libertad Llama a Resistir

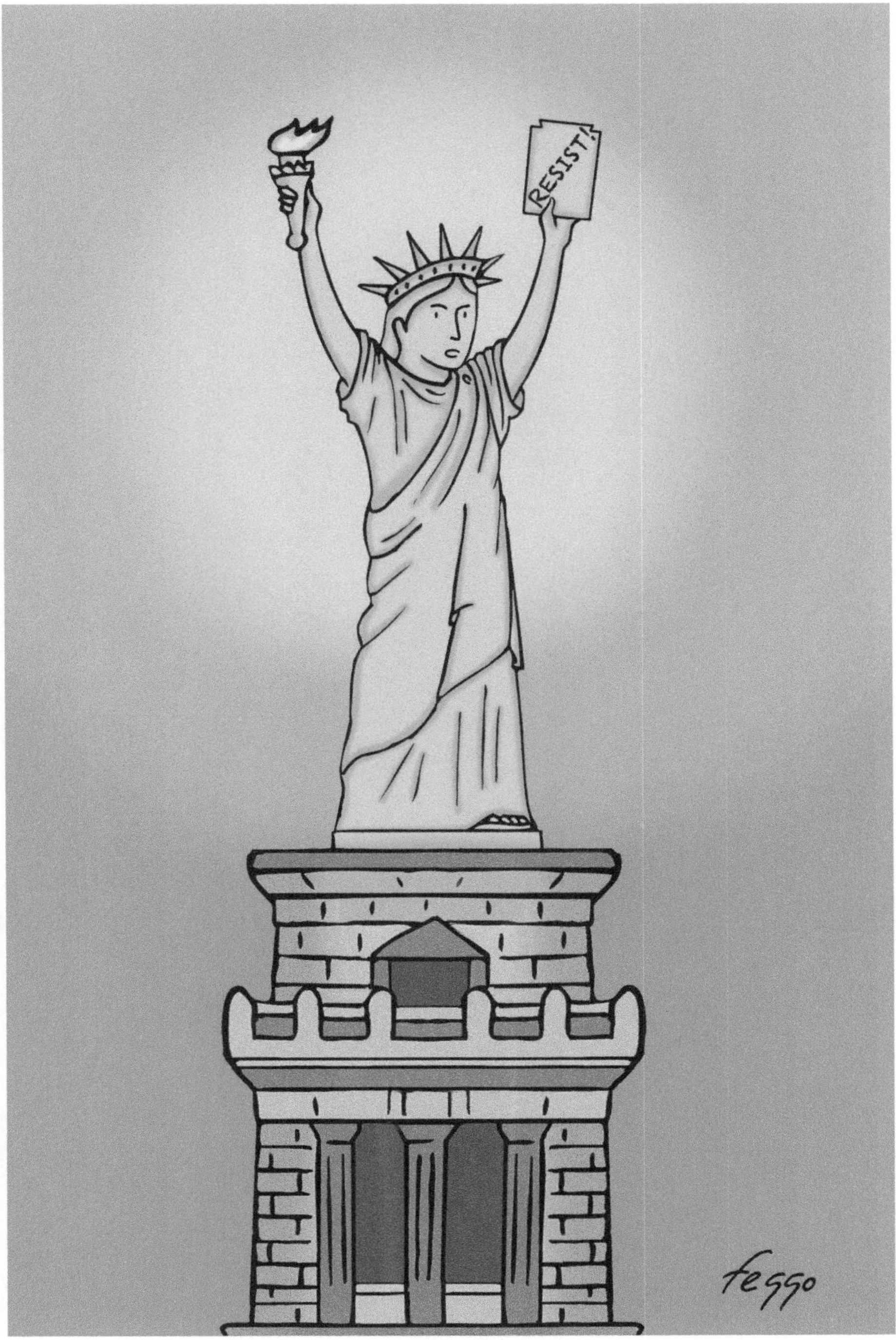
RESIST!
feggo

Liberty vs. The Border Patrol

Libertad Contra la Patrulla Fronteriza

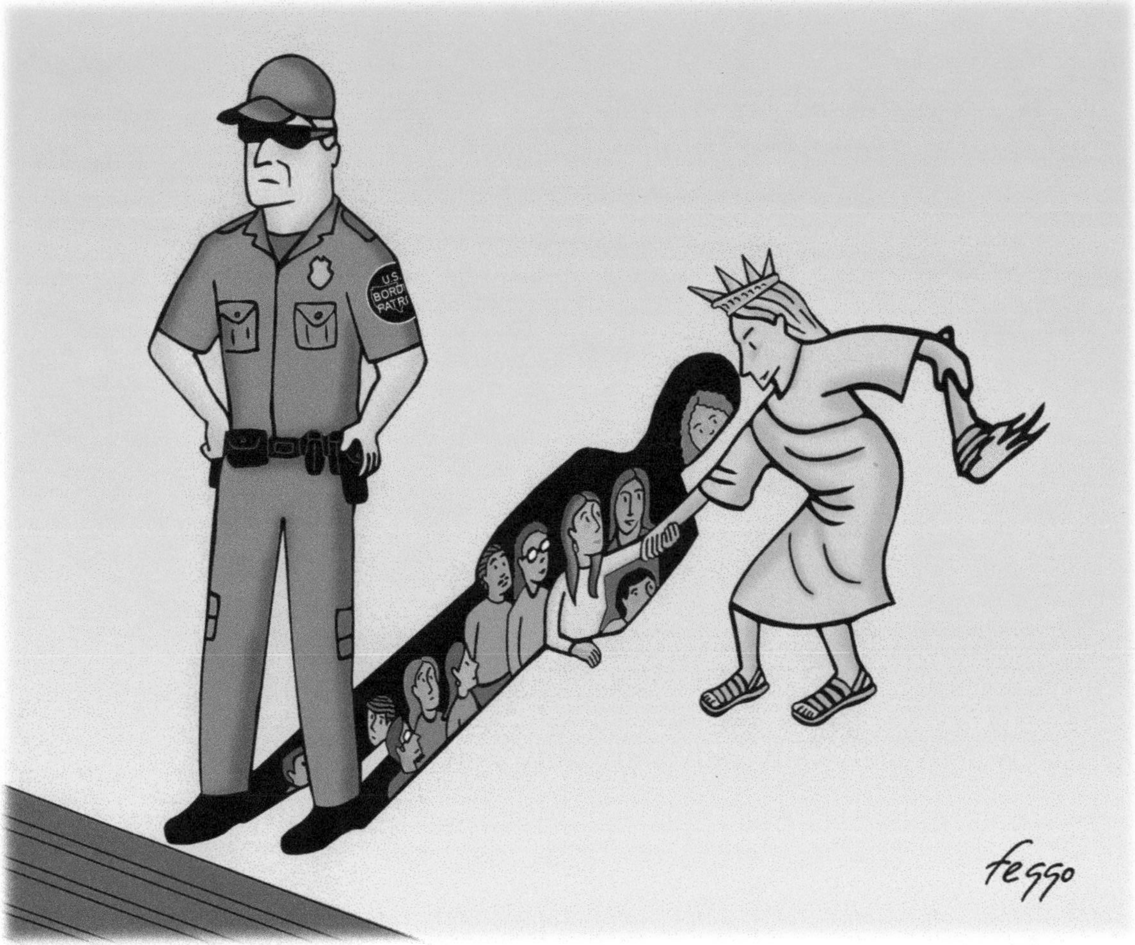
U.S.
BORD
PATR
feggo

**ICE (Immigration & Customs Enforcement)
Arrests Lady Liberty**

ICE (Control de Inmigración y Aduanas)
Arresta a la Dama Libertad

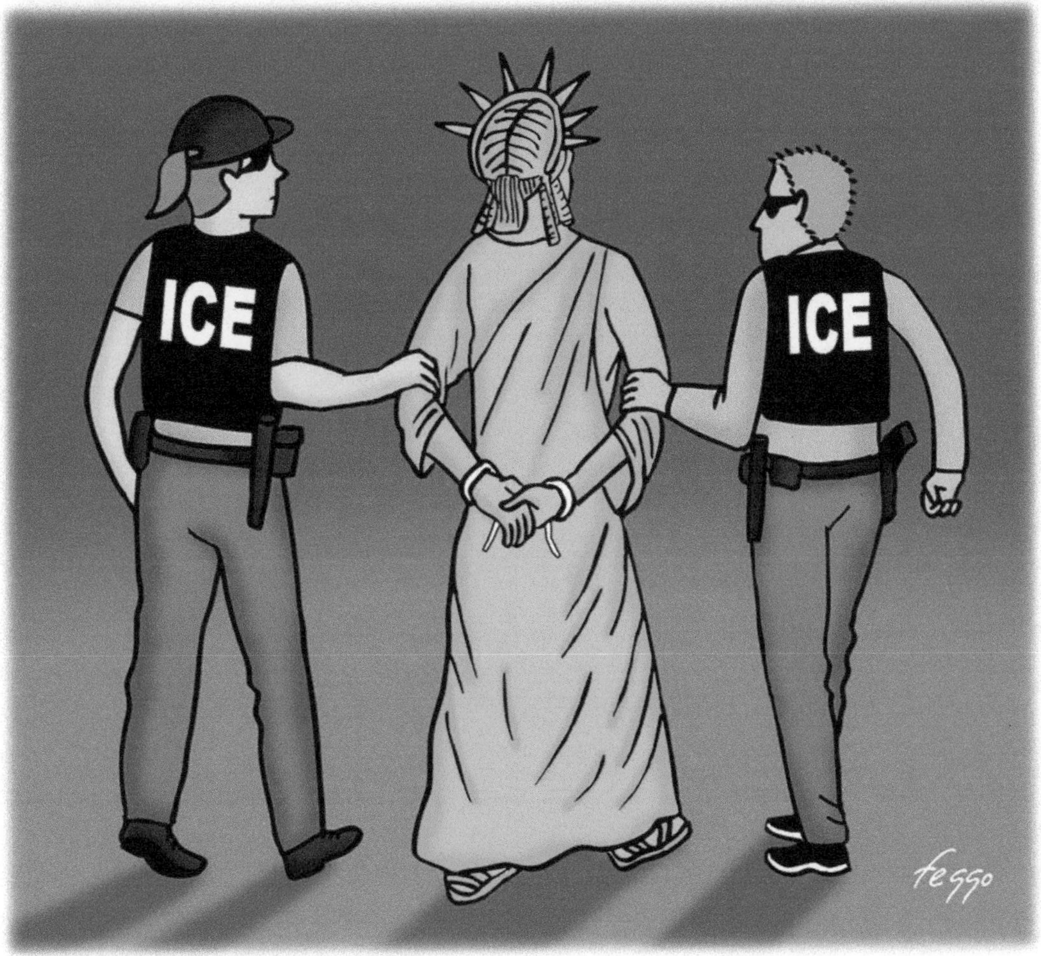
ICE
ICE
feggo

Rays of Hope

Hundreds of thousands of DREAMers (from Development, Relief and Education for Alien Minors) have been in a legal limbo since the bill's creation in 2001, and it was not until President Barack Obama turned it into an act on November 29, 2010, that they had a hope for a better future. About 740,000 DREAMers had registered by the end of 2012. On September 5, 2017, President Donald Trump rescinded the program, breaking his word that he cared for the Dreamers. Fortunately, on his first day in office on January 20, 2021, President Joseph Biden issued an executive order to preserve and fortify the program and pass legislation allowing them to apply for residency and providing them with a path to citizenship.

Rayos de Esperanza

Los DREAMers han estado en un limbo legal desde la creación del proyecto de ley en 2001 y no fue hasta que el presidente Barack Obama lo convirtió en ley el 29 de noviembre de 2010 que tenían la esperanza de un futuro mejor. Para fines del 2012, 740,000 personas se habían registrado para el programa. El 5 de septiembre de 2017, el presidente Donald Trump lo rescindió, rompiendo su palabra de proteger a los Dreamers. Afortunadamente, en su primer día en el cargo, el 20 de enero de 2021 el presidente Joseph Biden emitió una orden ejecutiva para preservar y fortalecer el programa y aprobar una legislación para solicitar la residencia y eventualmente también la ciudadanía.

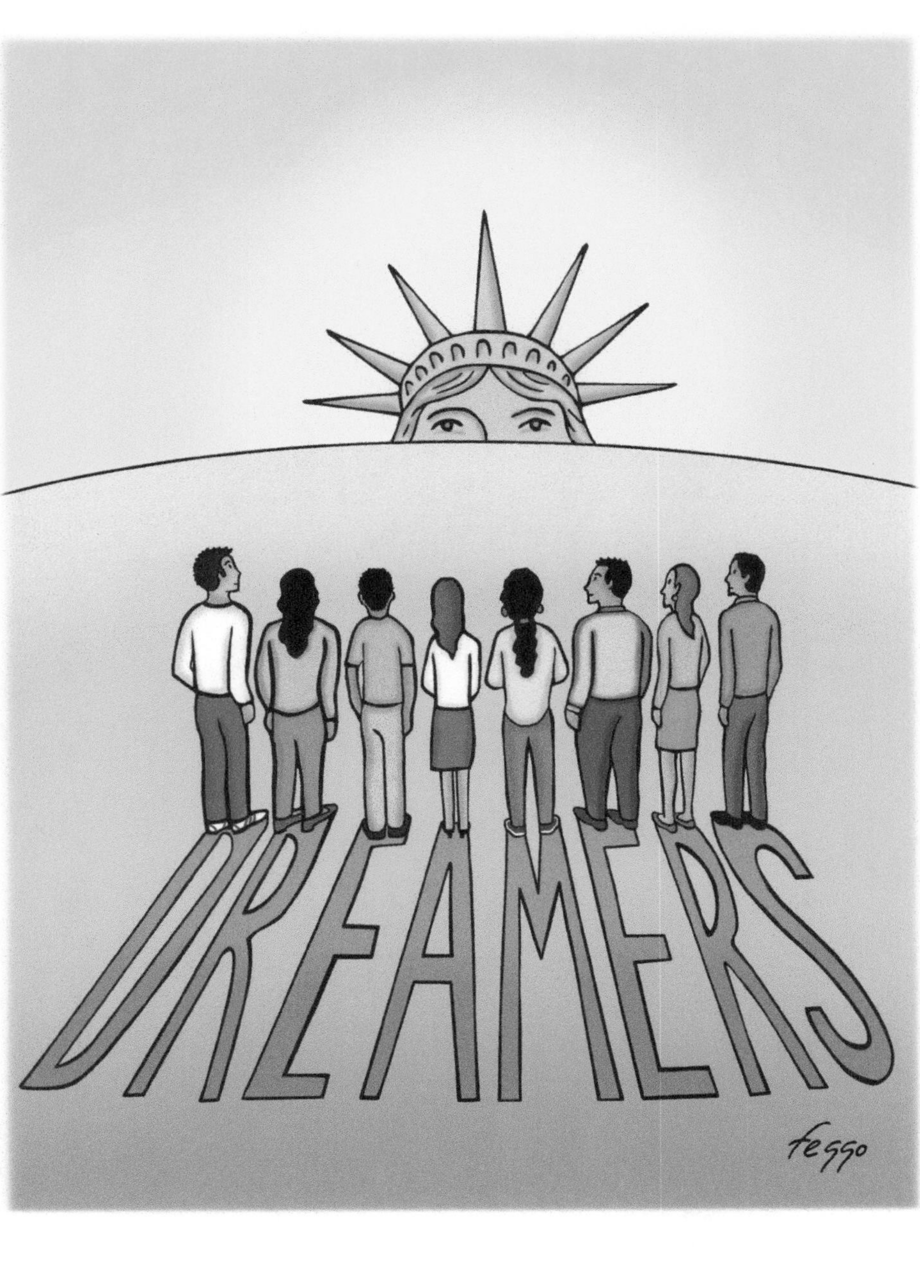
DREAMERS
feggo

**Thorny Welcome to Central American
Asylum Seekers**

Bienvenida Espinosa a los Centroamericanos
que Buscan Asilo Político

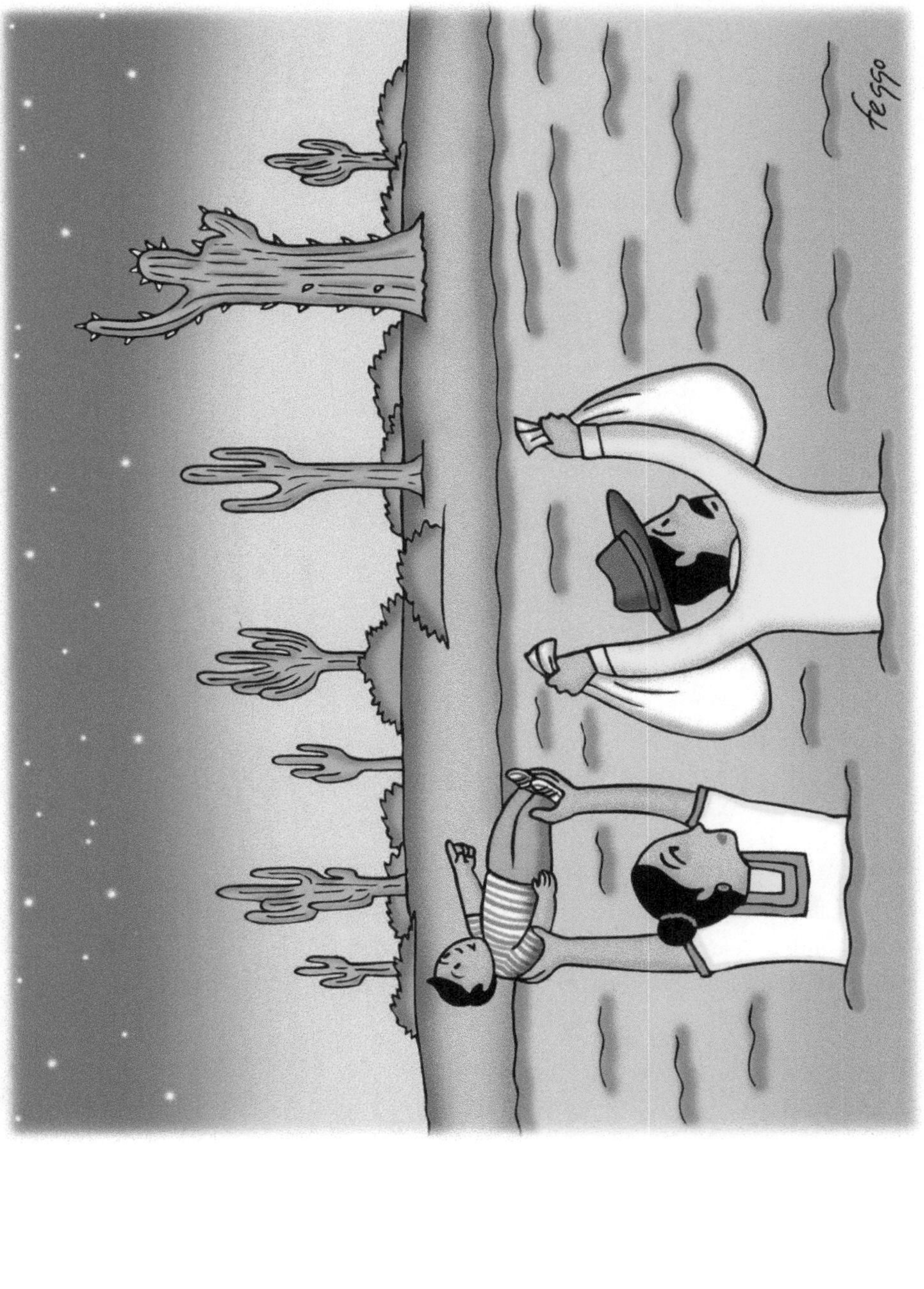

Undocumented Immigrants Serving Liberty

Unfortunately, many immigrants have been exploited in their search of the American Dream. For them serving Liberty has come at a high price.

Inmigrantes Indocumentados Sirviendo a la Libertad

Desafortunadamente, muchos inmigrantes han sido explotados durante su búsqueda del Sueño Americano, servir a la Libertad ha tenido un costo muy alto para ellos.

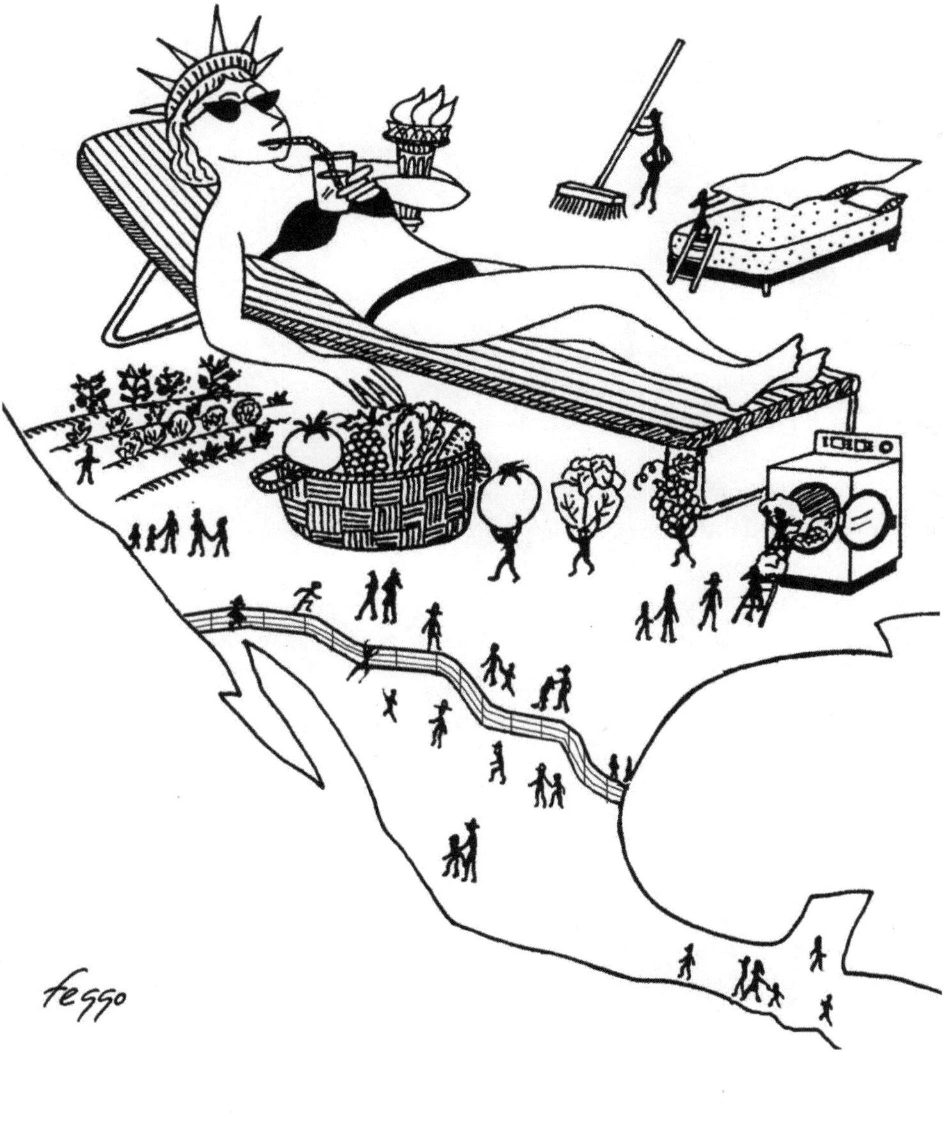
feggo

Trump's Liberty: Crown of Thorns

His administration's approach to immigration
violated basic human rights and enforced the
separation of children from their parents as a
punishment policy. It is ironic that Stephen Miller,
his far-right anti-immigration political advisor
and chief architect of the Muslim travel ban,
the refugees' admission reduction, and family
separation plan, has ancestors who escaped the
1903-1906 anti-Jewish pogroms in Russia and
came as immigrants to America.

La Libertad de Trump: Corona de Espinas

El enfoque en política migratoria de su
administración violó derechos humanos básicos
y aplicó la separación de niños de sus padres
como una política de castigo. Es irónico que su
asesor político de ultra derecha, Stephen Miller,
arquitecto principal de la prohibición de entrada
a musulmanes, la reducción a la admisión
de refugiados y la separación familiar, tenga
antepasados que escaparon de las persecuciones
a judíos en Rusia en 1903-06, llegando como
inmigrantes a este país.

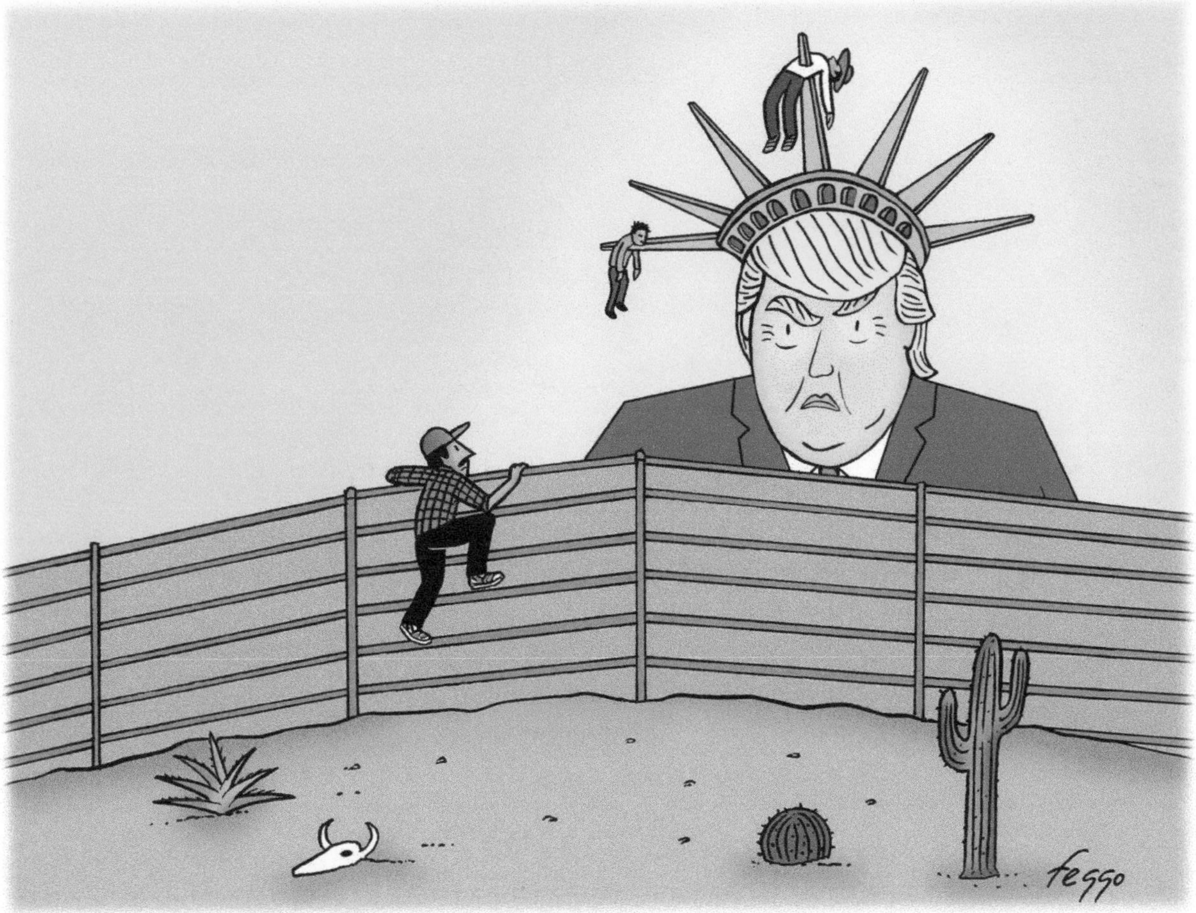
feggo

Trump's Government Shutdown

The longest government shutdown in U.S. history (12/18/2018-1/25/2019) was caused by his five billion dollar request to fund his southern border wall project which was denied by Congress.

Apagando Agencias del Gobierno

El cierre del gobierno más largo en la historia de los Estados Unidos (18/12/2018 25-1/1/2019) fue causado por el presidente por su solicitud de $5 mil millones para su proyecto del muro fronterizo. El Congreso rechazó el financiamiento.

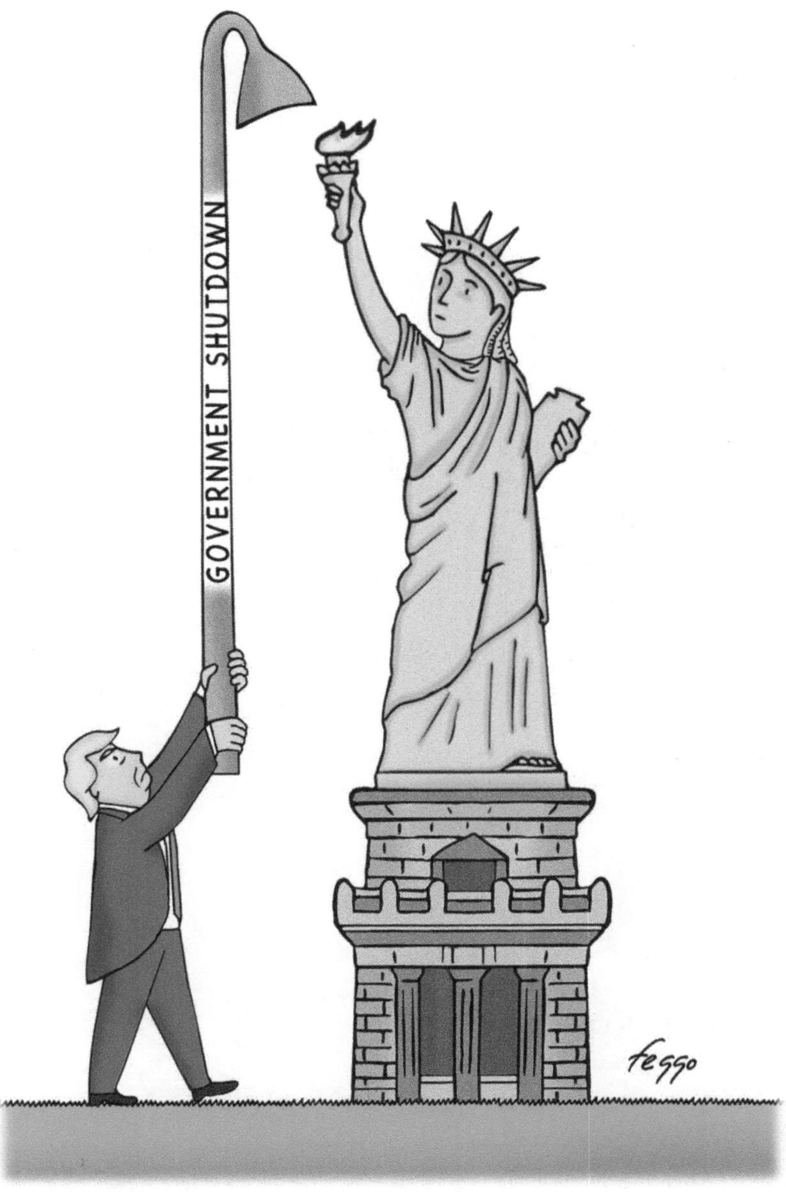
GOVERNMENT SHUTDOWN
feggo

Lady Liberty Receives Green Card Lottery's Applications from all Over the World (Diversity Visa Program)

La Dama Libertad Recibe Solicitudes, Provenientes de Todo el Mundo, Para la Lotería Anual de Tarjetas de Residencia Desde Todo el Mundo (Programa de Diversidad de Visas)

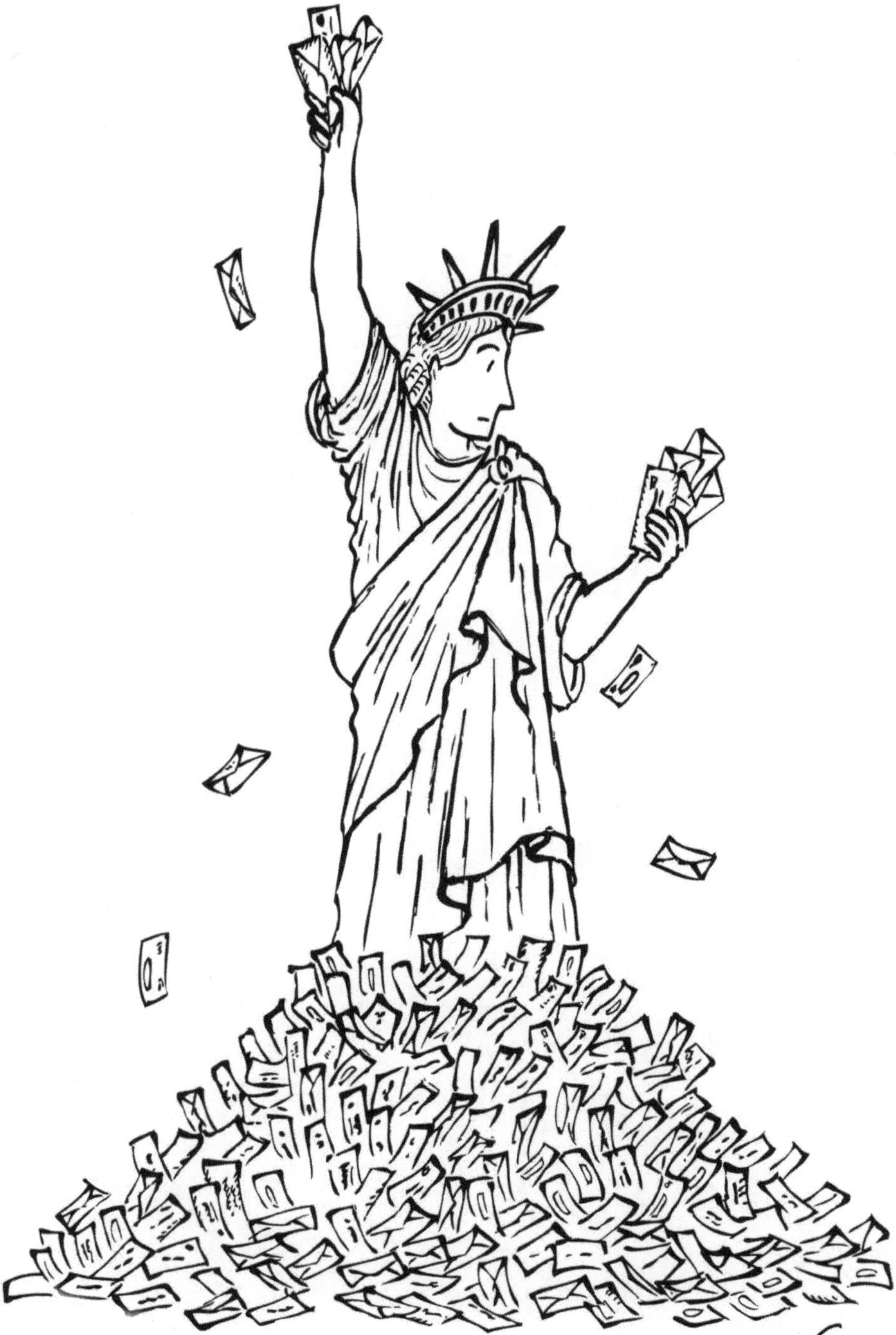
feggo

Different Values

Diferentes Valores

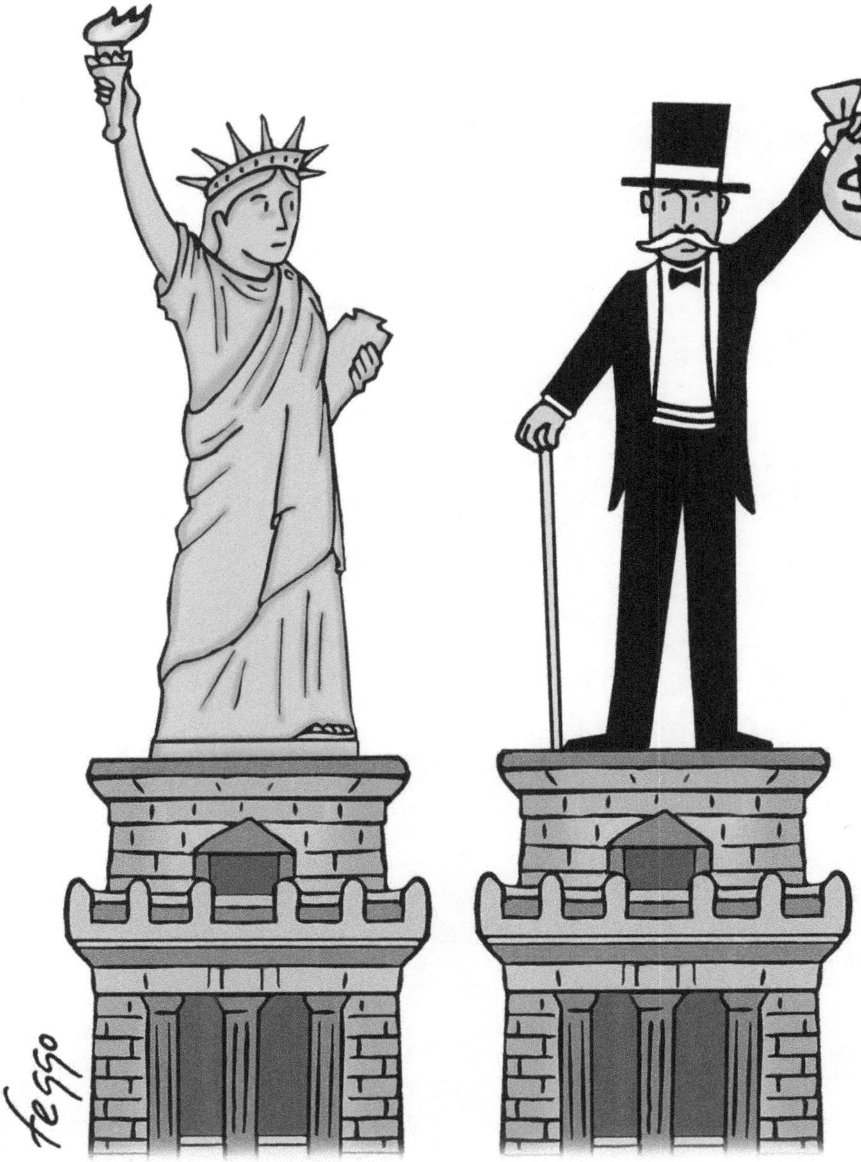
$
feggo

Zen Liberty: In Search of Peace and Quiet

Libertad Meditando: Buscando Paz y Calma

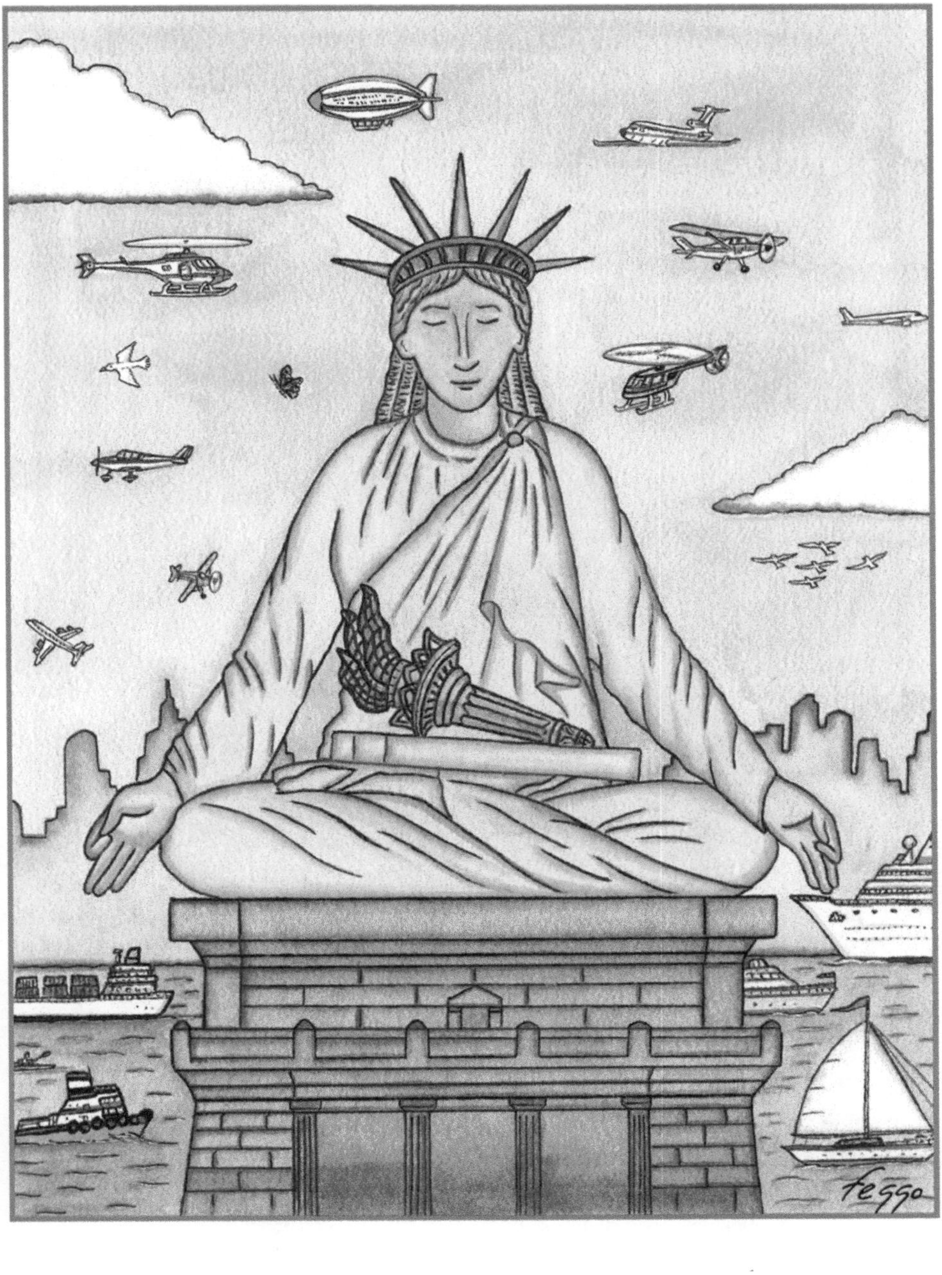
feggo

Taking Our Daughters to Work Day

Created in the summer of 1992 by the Ms. Foundation, it was later expanded to include boys in 2003 and later renamed Taking Our Children to Work Day. It is usually celebrated the third week in April.

Día de Llevar a Nuestras Hijas al Trabajo

Creado en el verano de 1992 por la Fundación Ms., se expandió en 2003 para incorporar a los hijos, y al final se renombró para incluir a hijos de cualquier género. Suele celebrarse en la 3a. semana de abril.

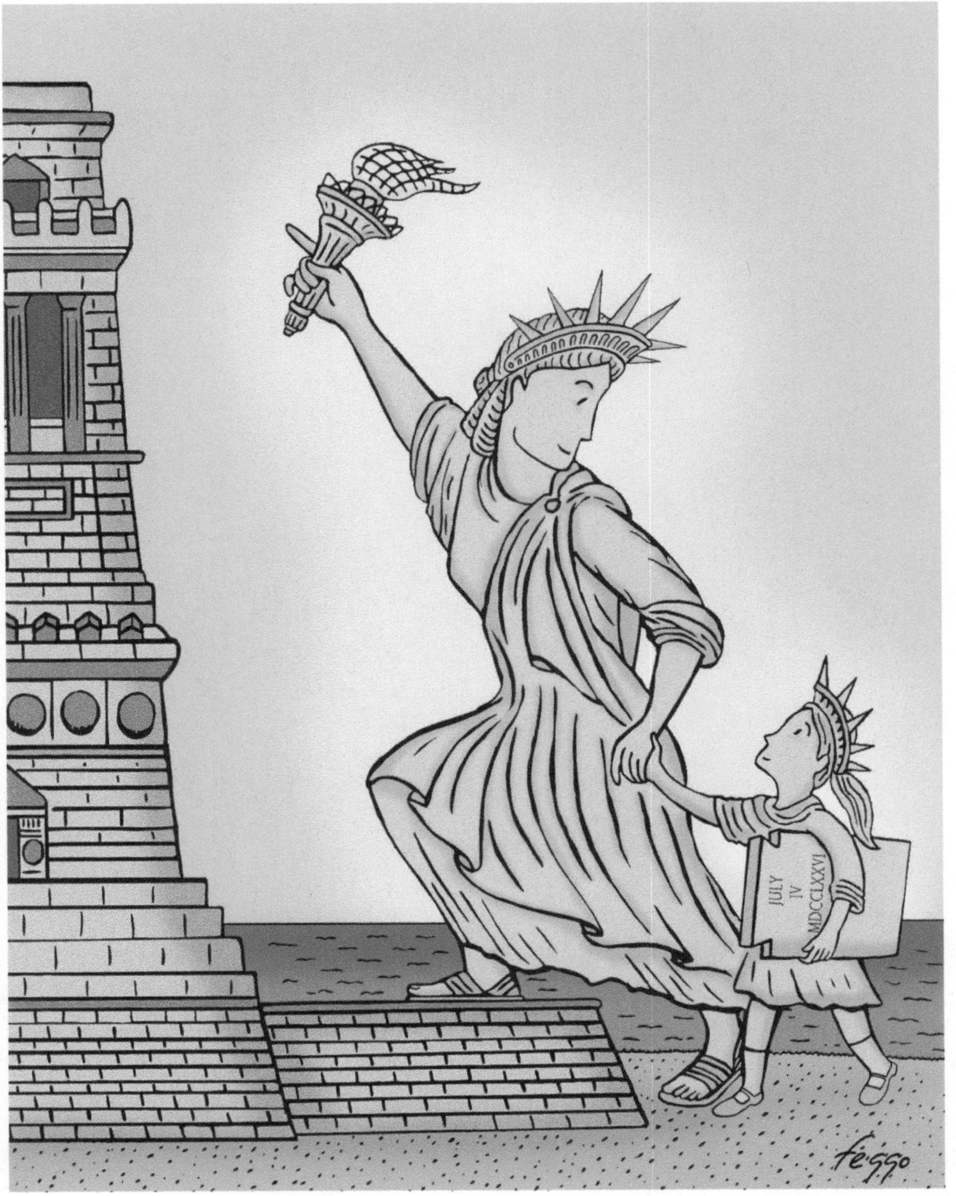
JULY
IV
MDCCLXXVI
feggo

Sharp Defense

In 1991 the US was the host of the third FIFA's Women World Cup. The US team has won the cup four times, out of eight celebrated so far.

Aguda Defensa

En 1991, Estados Unidos fue el anfitrión de la 3a Copa Mundial Femenina de la FIFA. La selección estadounidense ha ganado cuatro de las ocho copas celebradas hasta el momento.

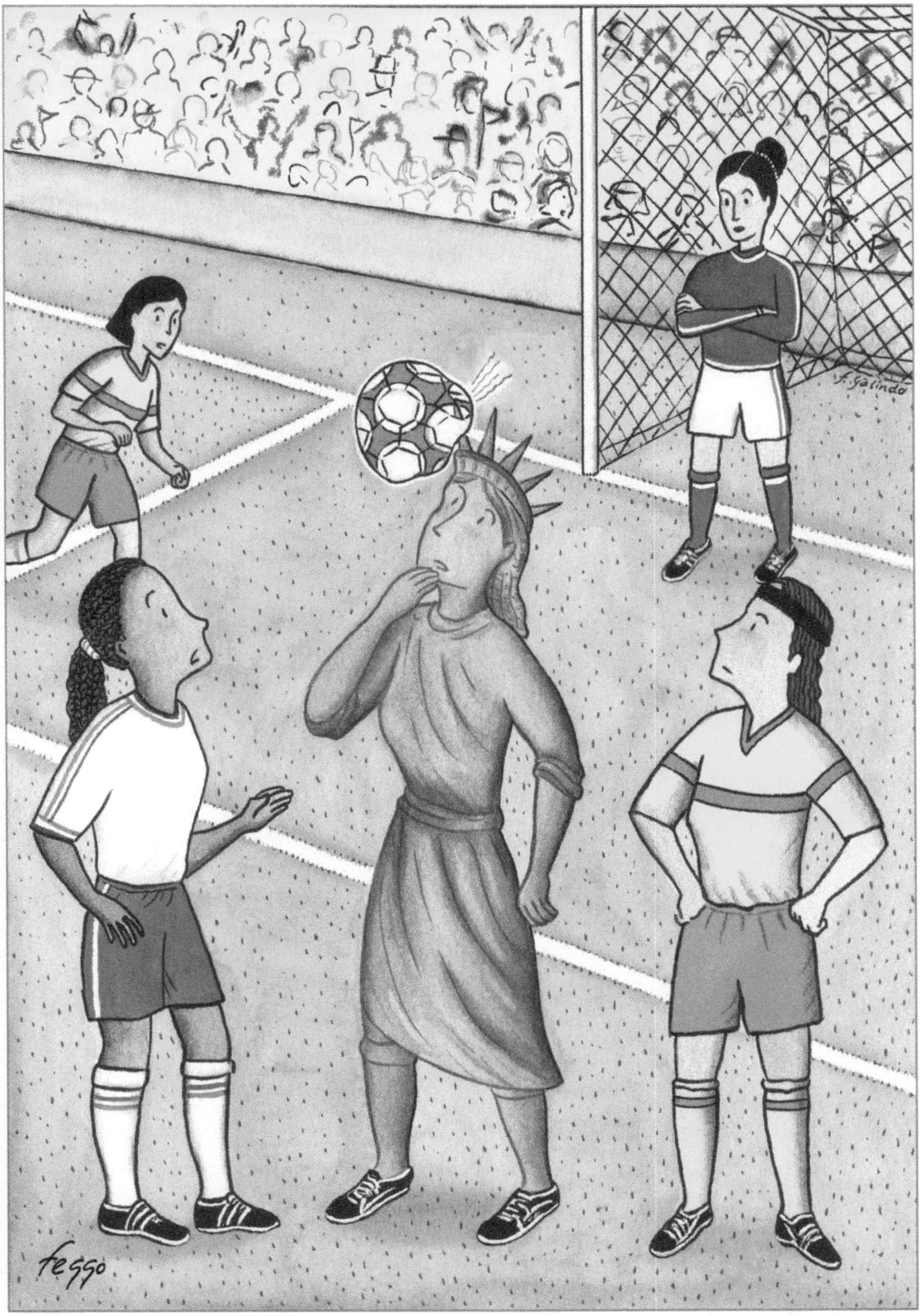
f. galindo
feggo

Liberty's Facebook

Lady Liberty posts her thoughts on social media about her experience during Superstorm Sandy, in the autumn of 2012.

La Dama Libertad comparte sus pensamientos en las redes sociales, acerca de su experiencia durante la supertormenta Sandy, en el otoño del 2012.

Facebook 2 8 Home

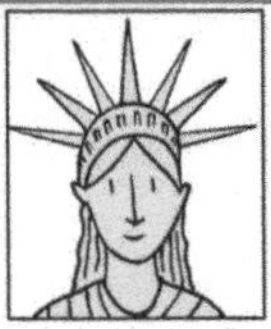

Lady Liberty
Edit Profile

What's on your mind?

Lady Liberty commented on her activity:

My Facebook page asks me what's on my mind.

Really? Well, thanks for the invitation to share my thoughts, nobody ever asked me before! I've been at this place day after day since October 28, 1886, with one arm raising a torch, the other holding up a tablet that by now I wish was an iPad. On top of staying in that position indefinitely, tourists are always crawling inside me -- up and down, down and up like ants! I wish I could actually digest some of them. Coming from all over the world they might actually be delicious. Italians, Mexicans, French, Greeks, Japanese, you name it -- an international smogasbord!
They also take photos, hundreds per second! If only I could get paid one cent per photo and I'd be able to go on vacation. How many photos have I appeared in? More than Lady Gaga? My favorite is that one with John Lennon.
In any case, I have also been a great spectator -- the ultimate bystander -- watching how this land has slowly changed since I first stood tall. My saddest day was being a witness to the September 11 attacks. That day I desperately wished I could do something -- if only I could've moved to stop those planes.
I am also very proud of being a symbol of Freedom and of hope for countless immigrants who have come to these shores. I was proud of my walk-on -- I mean, cameo -- role in The Godfather, when little Vito Corleone was at Ellis Island waiting his turn to be admitted into the USA.
I am also a souvenir. What an irony, all those little replicas of me are made in China! China of all places, not exactly a country known for its Liberty. I bet a lot of those workers would qualify as your tired, poor, huddled masses yearning to breathe free.
Let's talk about a subject which is a daily preoccupation for me and all true New Yorkers: the weather. Aside from the 9/11 attacks or some of the tacky outfits on the tourists, nothing really freaked me out...until Sandy. Boy, that was quite a storm, or Superstorm. Some people called it a tropical cyclone, hurricane, Category 3 storm, post-tropical cyclone with hurricane-force winds, whatever. Sandy was the mother of a hundred El Niños!

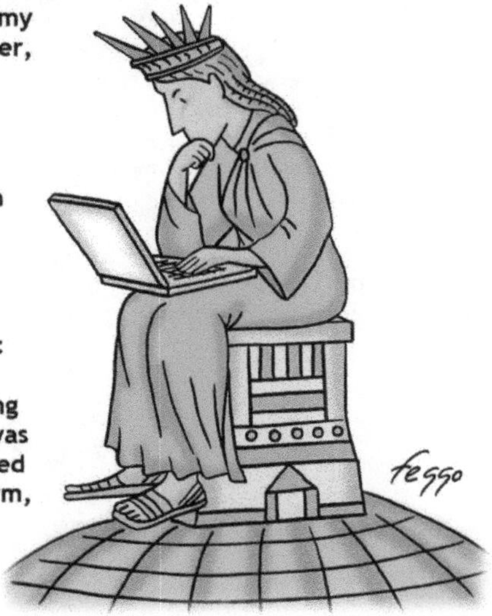
feggo

What's on your mind?

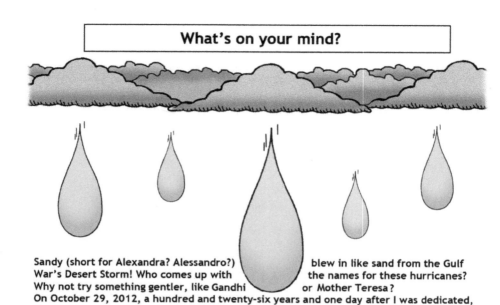

Sandy (short for Alexandra? Alessandro?) blew in like sand from the Gulf War's Desert Storm! Who comes up with the names for these hurricanes? Why not try something gentler, like Gandhi or Mother Teresa? On October 29, 2012, a hundred and twenty-six years and one day after I was dedicated, Sandy came ashore near Brigantine, NJ., just north of Atlantic City.

The storm had left a path of destruction through Jamaica, Cuba, the Bahamas, Haiti, Puerto Rico and the Dominican Republic. In the US it drenched 24 states, from Florida to Maine. It saved the most severe damage for New York and New Jersey. It left 147 fatalities and $75 billion in damages.

That day I felt, "this is it!" Forget Al-Qaeda's plans to blow me up. This was Mother Nature we are talking about. Does Lady Liberty stand a chance against Mother Nature? No siree! It didn't help that I'm a UNESCO World Heritage Site. I wanted to show my membership card and see if I could be spared, but it was no insurance against an act of God.
When the fierce wind began to blow, I was picturing myself at the end of the original Planet Of The Apes, when Charlton Heston finds my half-buried remains. Even Chuck's NRA guns couldn't stop Mother Nature, but I wished he could have made like Moses and controlled the tide that was splashing up my skirt. It felt like the Red Sea's waves were crashing down on New York Harbor!

There were bad omens before Sandy arrived: the storm would hit us during a full moon, and with the tide at its peak all the "unthinkable" scenarios could come true. Plus there were all those Maya doomsday predictions. What's next, I thought, an IRS audit?

What's on your mind?

Are these signs of the new times? Apparently yes. All these events lead me to think about the search for life's meaning, for a greater understanding. Our world is changing -- correction, humankind is abruptly changing it. It is crucial for your species to be aware that it is part of a larger planetary community. What you do here affects the whole world and vice versa.

The infamous Global Warming -- a term that even a toddler knows by now -- is a fact of life and, now, death. Unfortunately, there will likely be plenty of Sandys and Irenes in our future. Humankind has a very short memory.

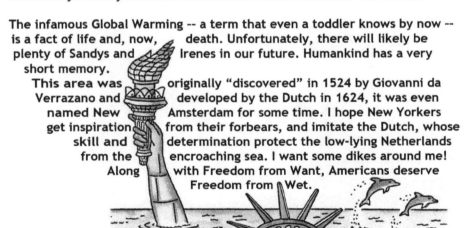

This area was originally "discovered" in 1524 by Giovanni da Verrazano and developed by the Dutch in 1624, it was even named New Amsterdam for some time. I hope New Yorkers get inspiration from their forbears, and imitate the Dutch, whose skill and determination protect the low-lying Netherlands from the encroaching sea. I want some dikes around me! Along with Freedom from Want, Americans deserve Freedom from Wet.

Cultural Encounters

Image commissioned by the Mexican Cultural
Institute of New York.

Encuentros Culturales

Imágen comisionada por el Instituto Cultural
Mexicano de Nueva York.

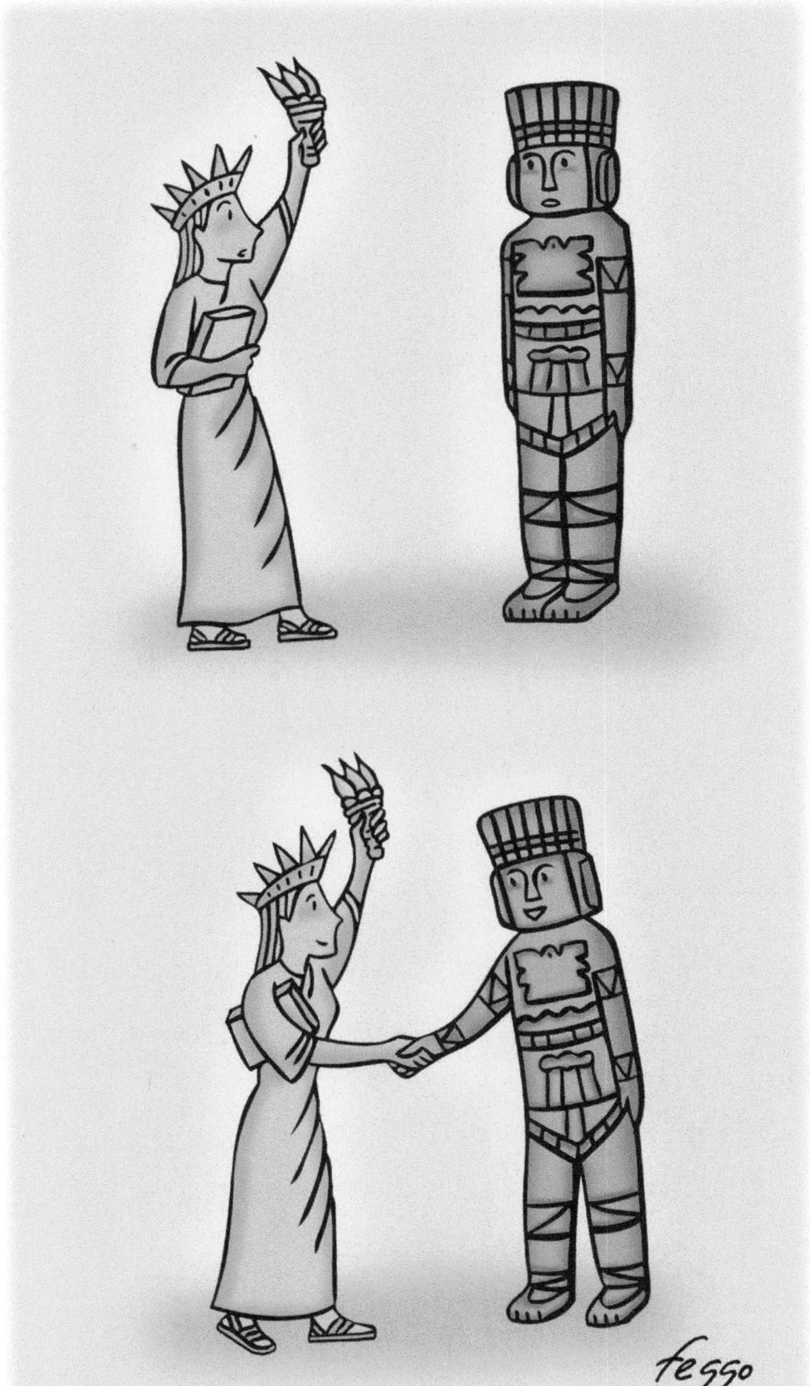
feggo

Miracle in Manhatitlan

An Aztec dancer transforms Lady Liberty into Lady of Guadalupe on her celebration day, December 12. Guadalupe is a very significant cultural symbol for Latin-Americans, like Lady Liberty is for Americans.

Milagro en Manhatitlan

Un danzante azteca transforma a la Estatua de la Libertad en La Virgen de Guadalupe, el día de su celebración, el 12 de diciembre. Ella es para los latinoamericanos un símbolo de suma importancia cultural como lo es Lady Liberty para los estadounidenses.

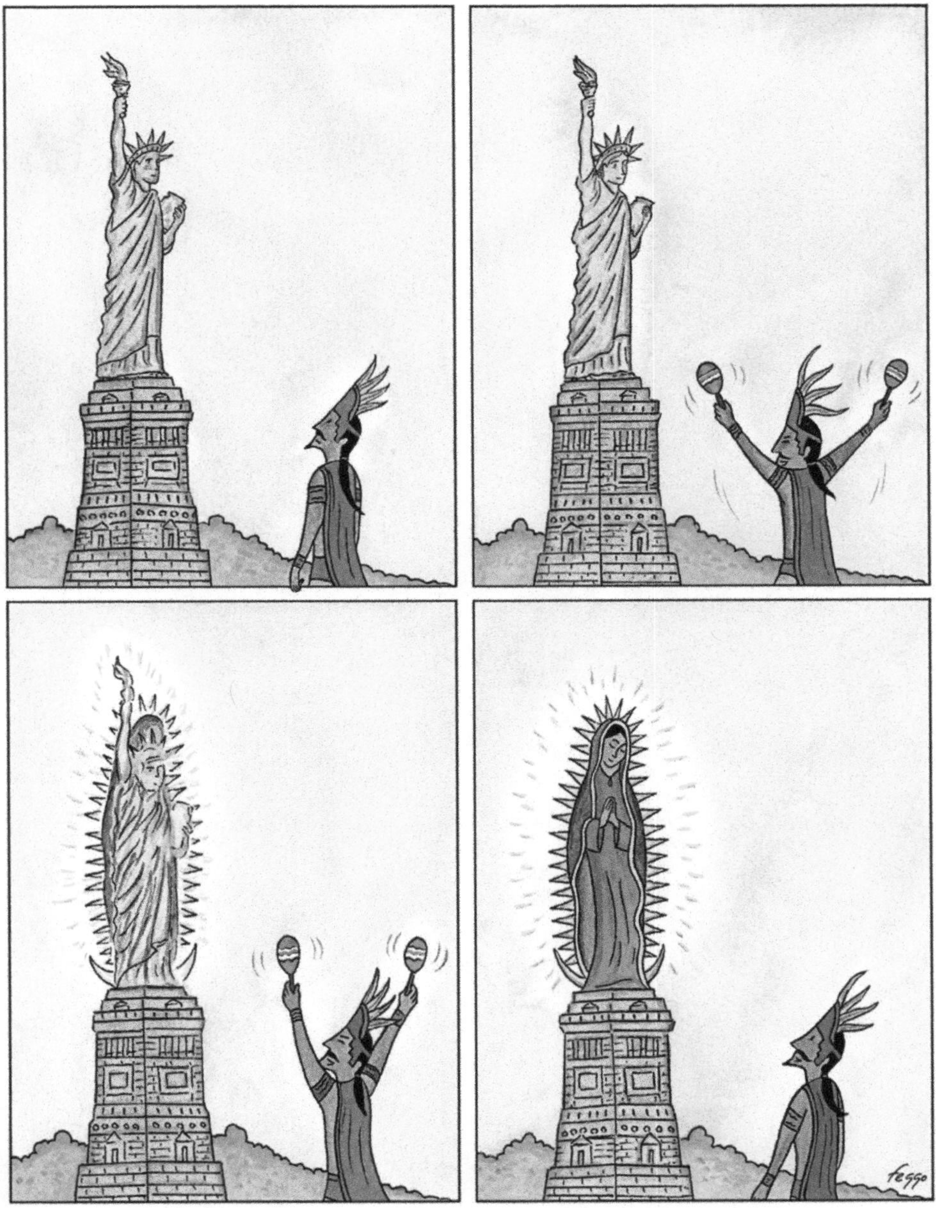
feggo

Times Square Dance with Frida Kahlo

Bailando con Frida Kahlo en Times Square

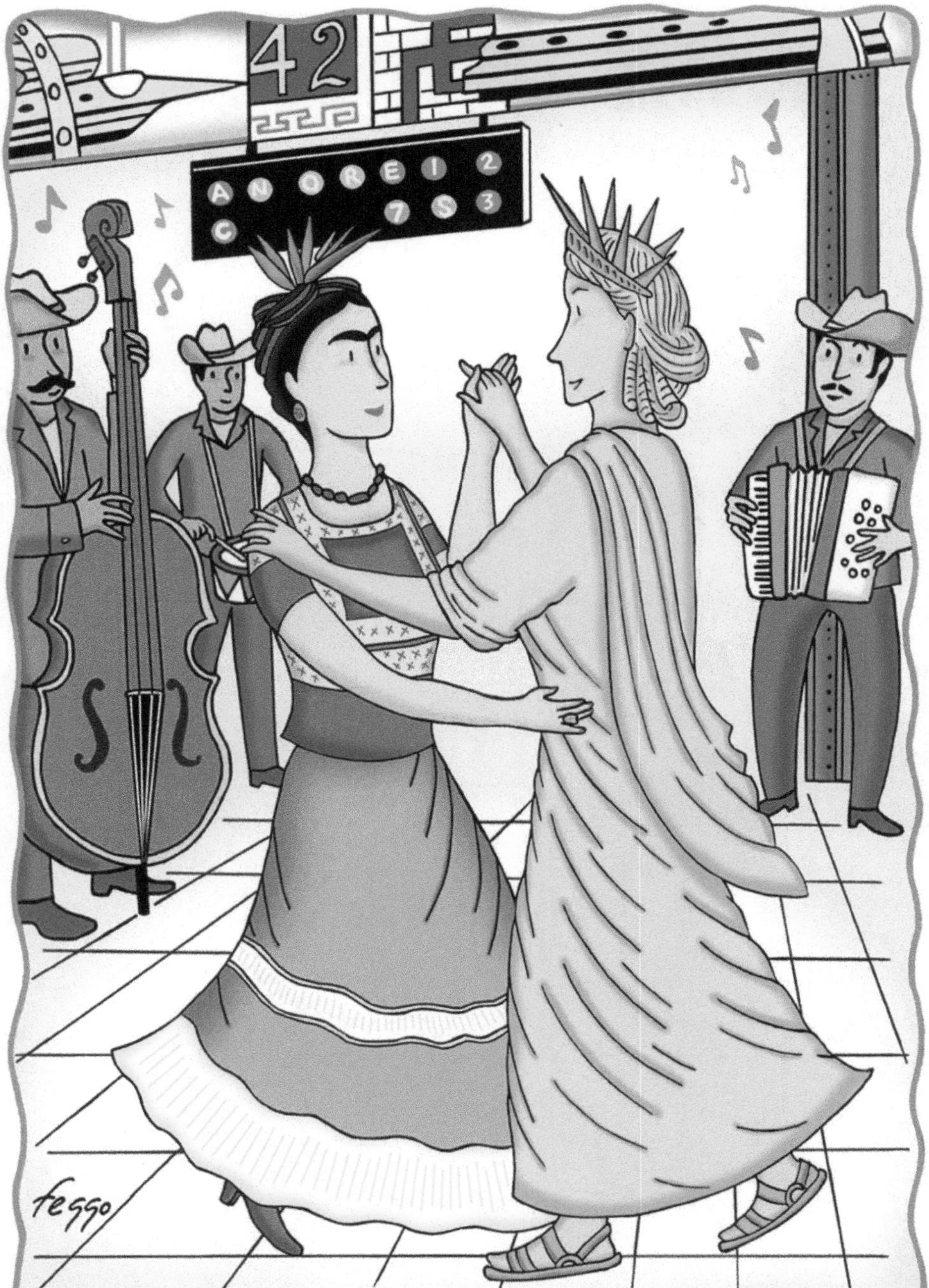
42
A N R E 1 2
C 7 3
feggo

Taking Liberties
Animation Project

Tomarse Libertades
Proyecto de Animación

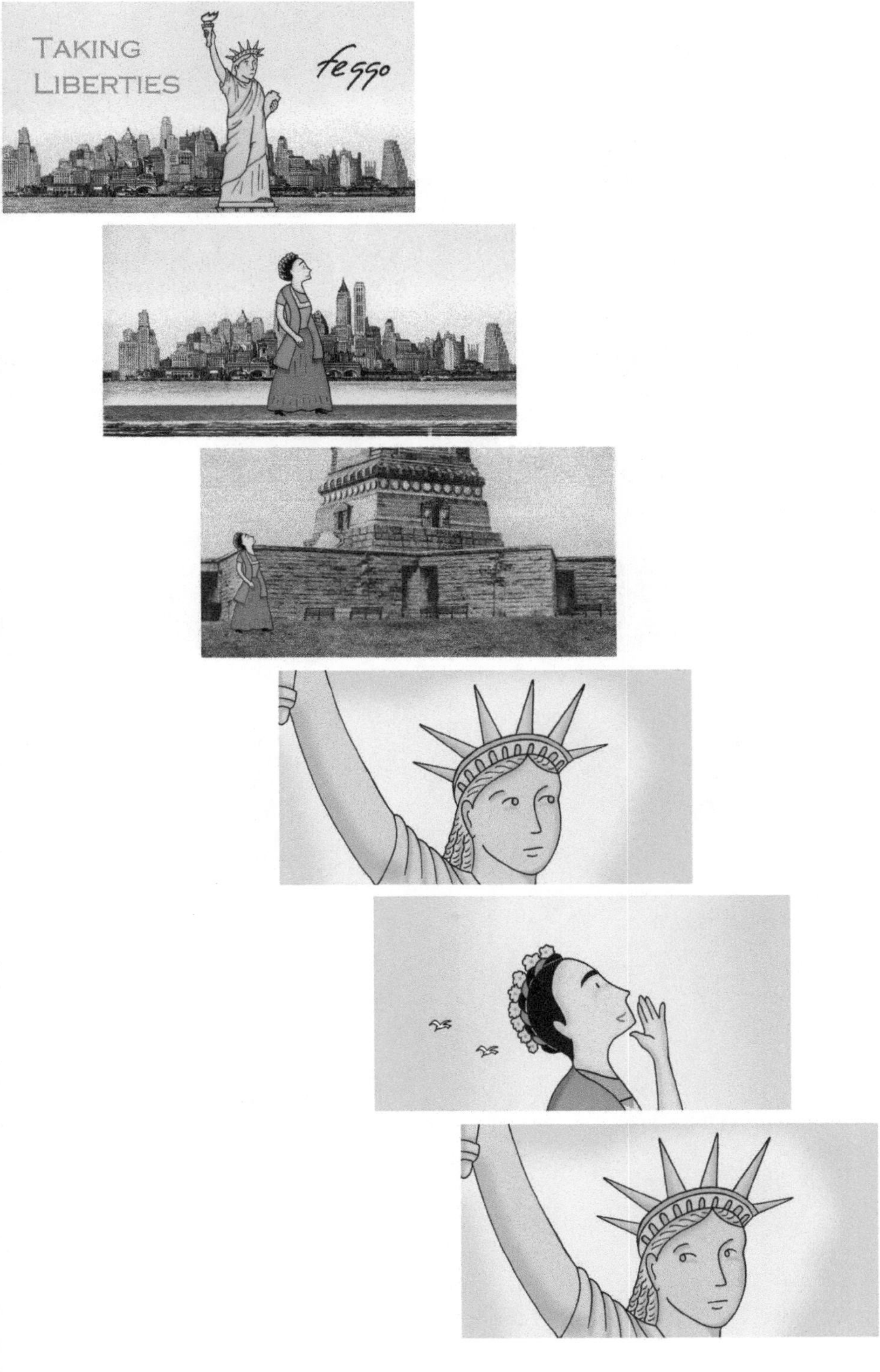
TAKING LIBERTIES
feggo

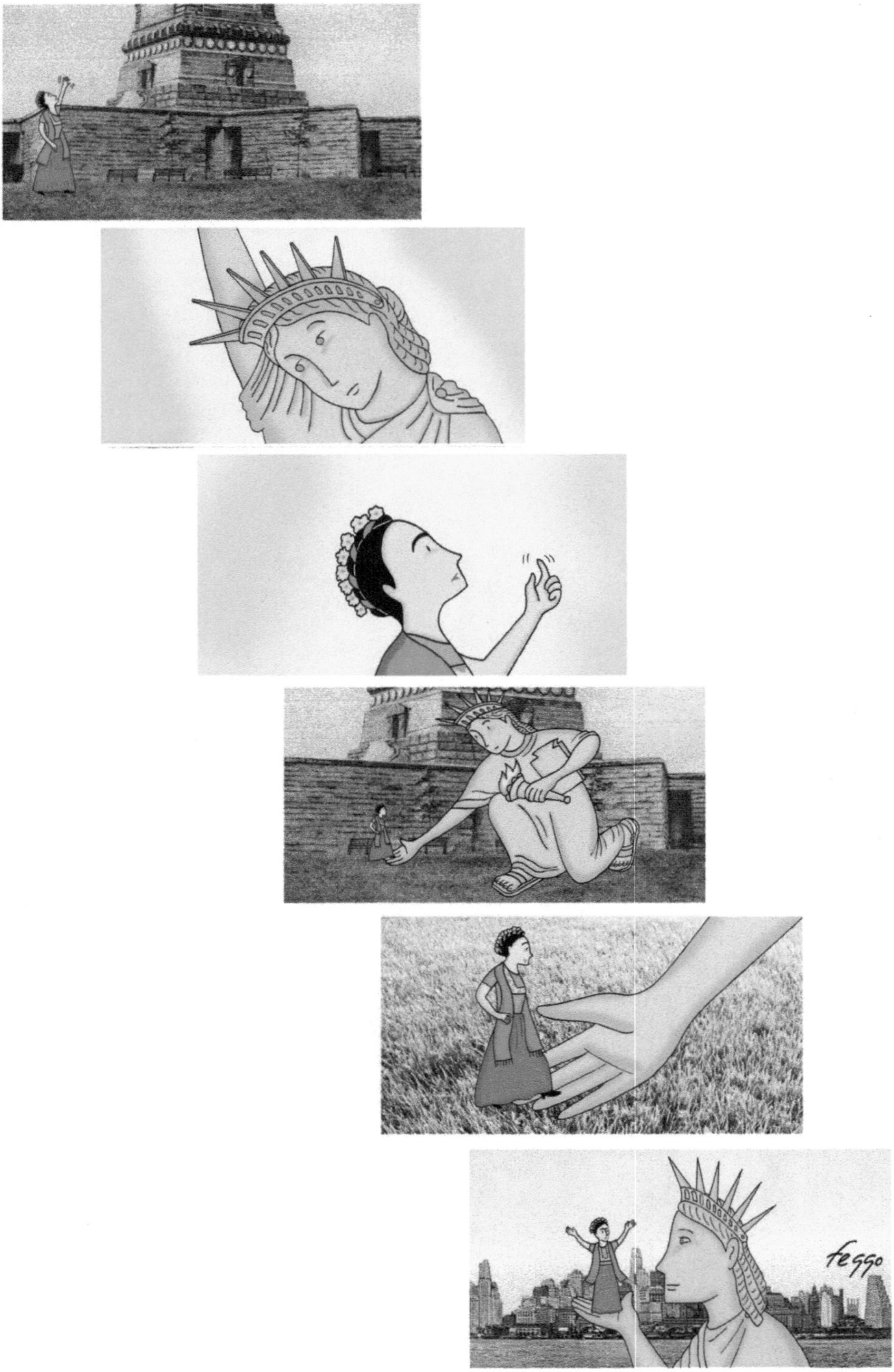
feggo

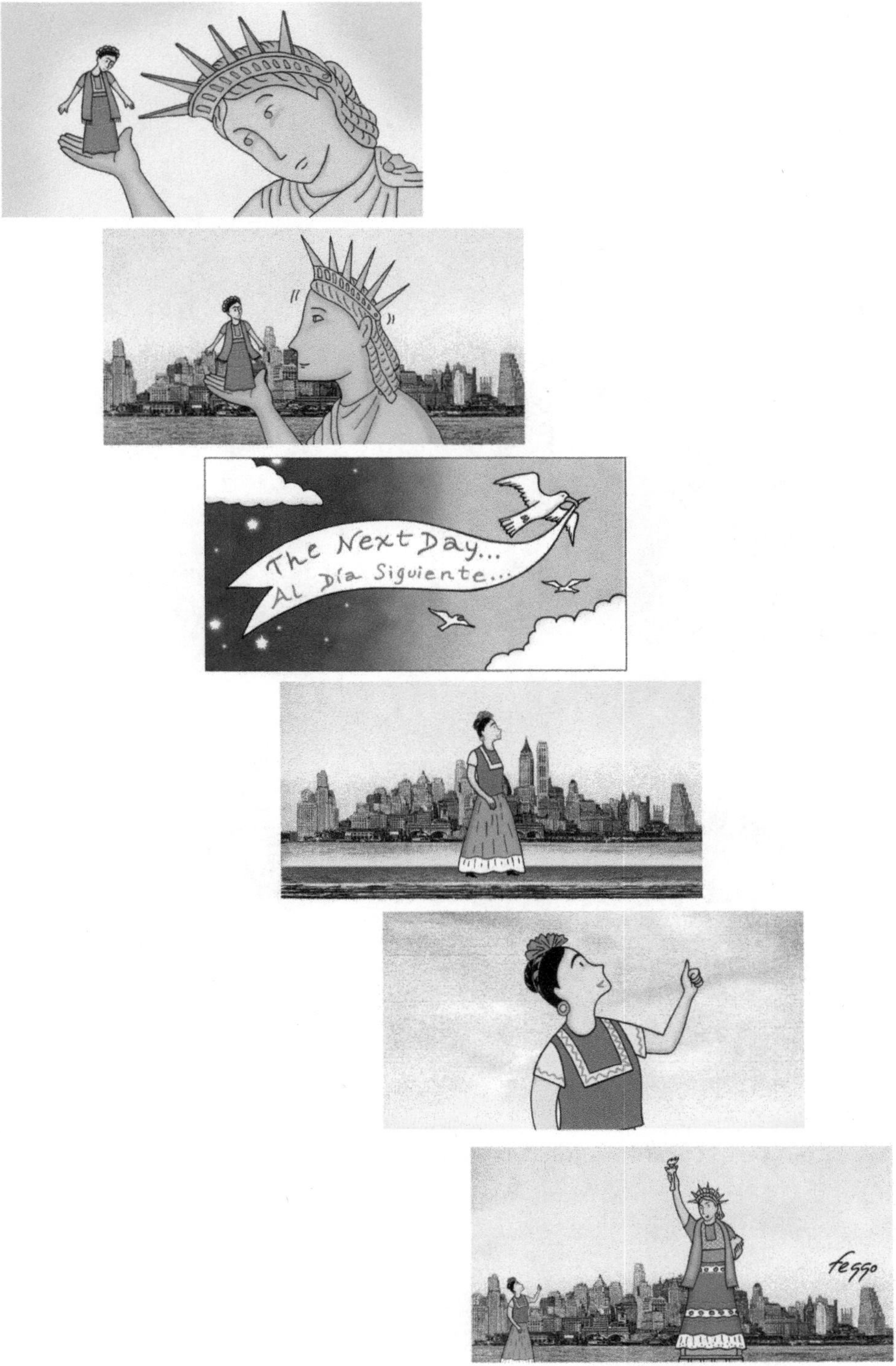
The Next Day...
Al Día Siguiente...
feggo

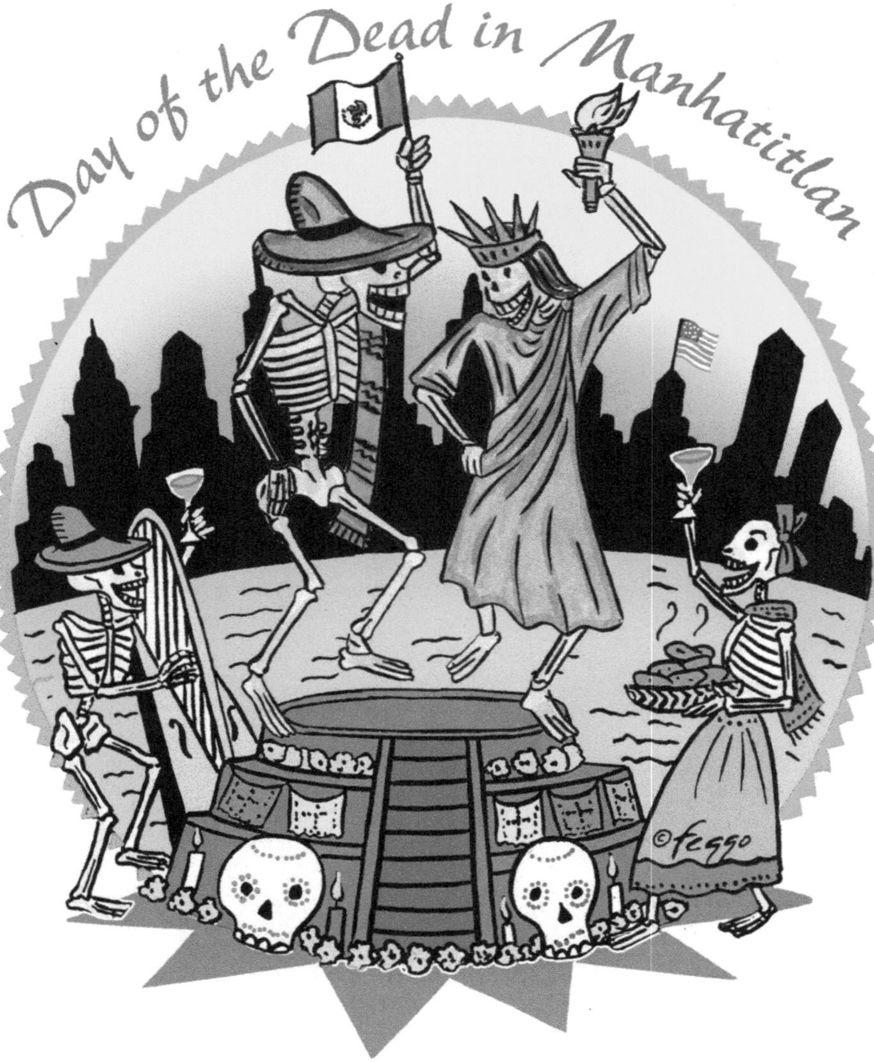
Day of the Dead in Manhatitlan
©feggo

Day of the Dead Celebration in Manhatitlan

Inspired by the etchings of Mexican artist José Guadalupe Posada.
(Early version this page and final version next page.)

Celebrando el Día de Muertos en Manhatitlan

Inspirado en la obra del grabador mexicano José Guadalupe Posada.
(Versión inicial en esta página y versión final en la siguiente página.)

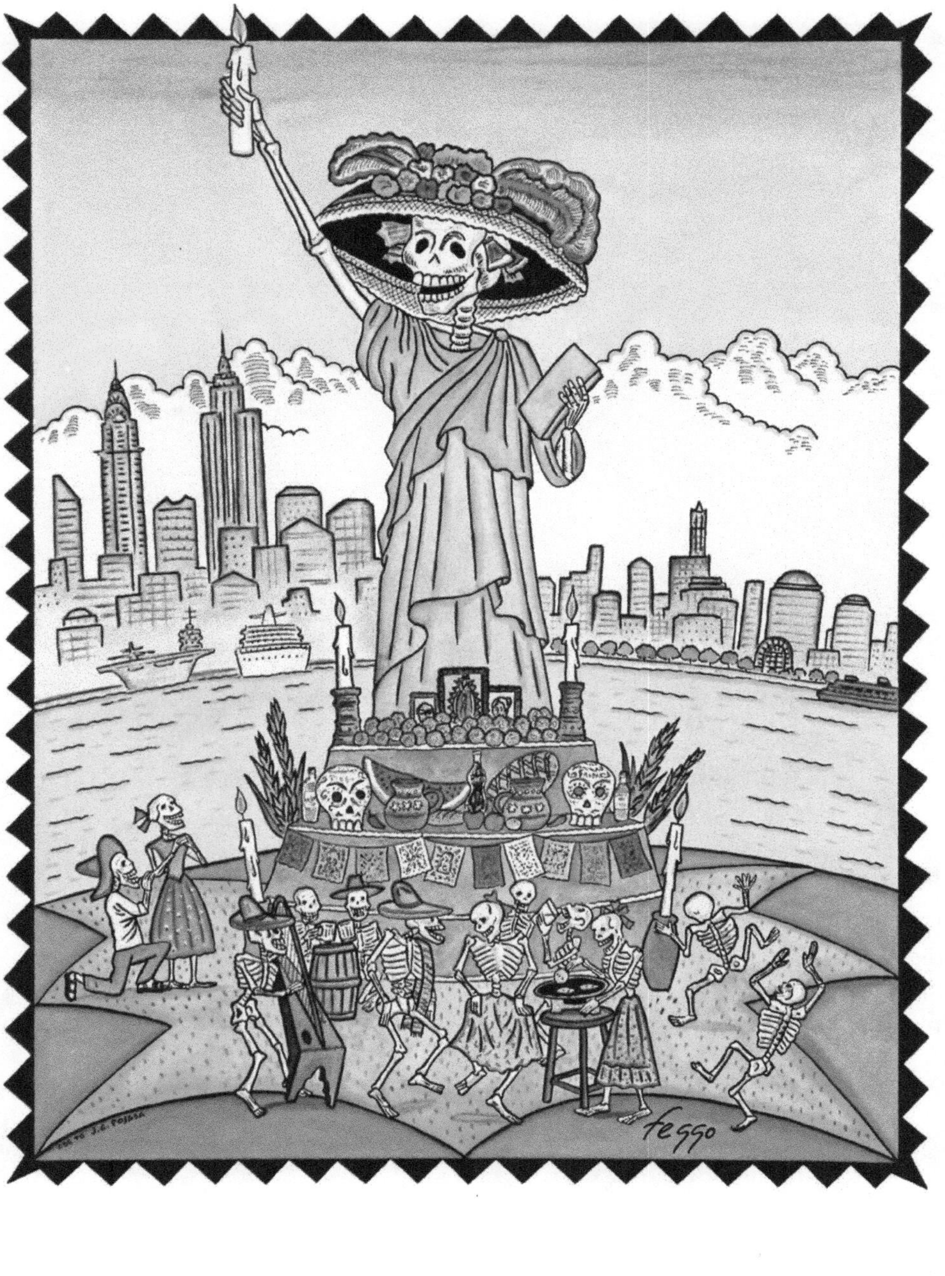
feggo

U.S.A. and Uruguay Friendship

Commissioned by the State Department and
the American Embassy in Uruguay, during the
Obama Administration. Collection of Uruguay's
President Jose Mujica.

Amistad Entre Estados Unidos y Uruguay

Obra comisionada por el Departmento de Estado
y la Embajada Americana de Uruguay, durante la
administración del Presidente Obama. Colección
del Presidente de Uruguay José Mujica.

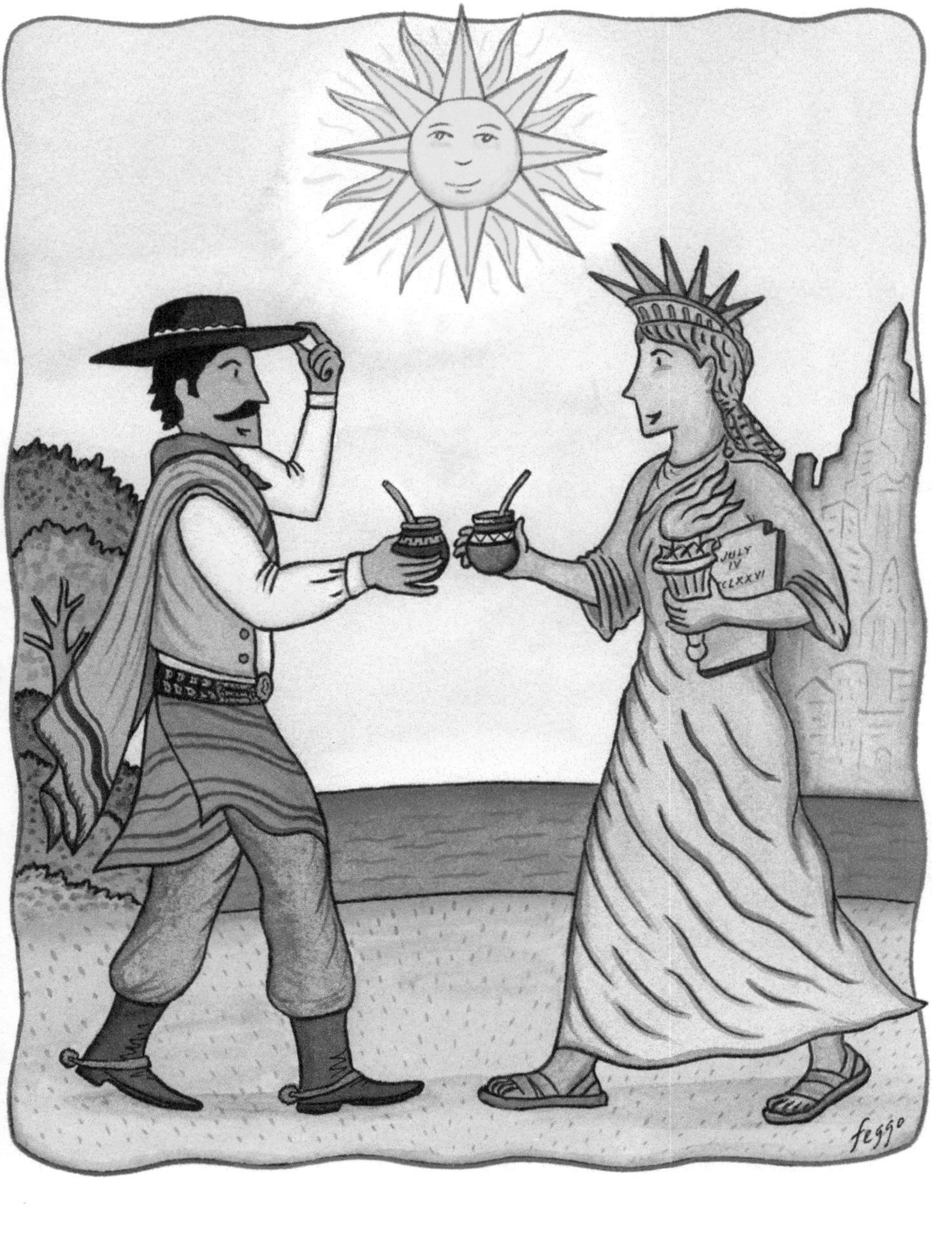
JULY
IV
CLXXVI
feggo

Mexican Independence Day Dance
Image commissioned by the Mexican Consulate
in New York for the Mexican Independence Day
Celebration on September 15.

Danza de La Independencia
Imágen comisionada por el Consulado Mexicano
de Nueva York, para la celebración de La
Independencia de México, el 15 de septiembre.

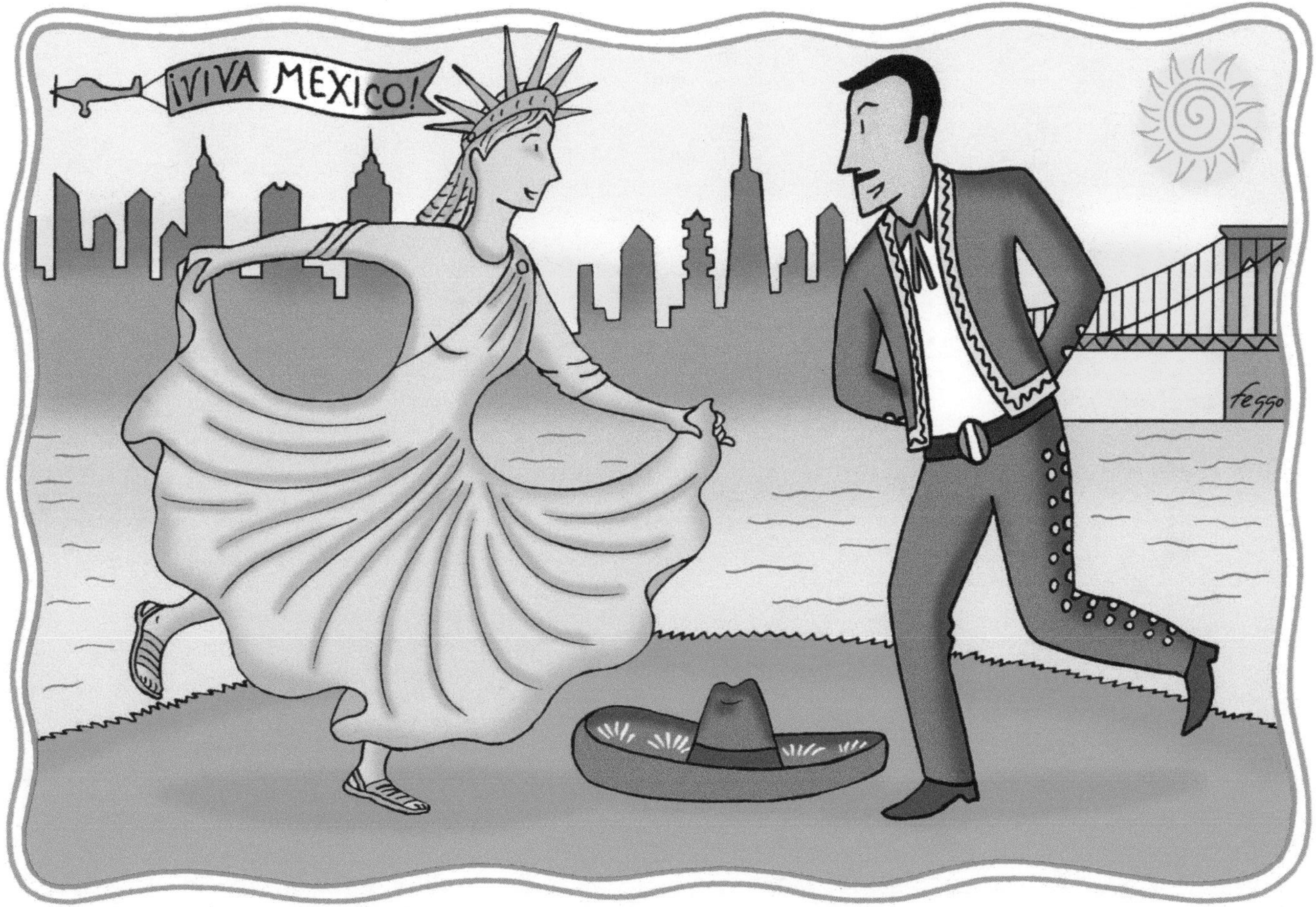
¡VIVA MEXICO!
feggo

Venus de Milo's Day Dream

A playful take on two famous sculptures.

El Sueño de la Venus de Milo

Lo que imagina la famosa escultura.

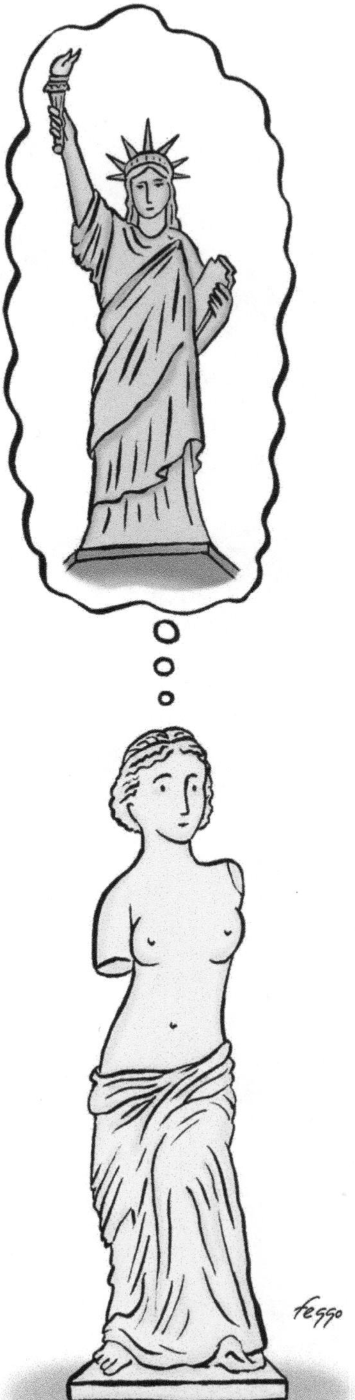
feggo

Vegetarian Thanksgiving Celebration

Celebración Vegetariana del Día de Acción
de Gracias

Legalizing Marijuana in New York

Legalizando Marihuana en Nueva York

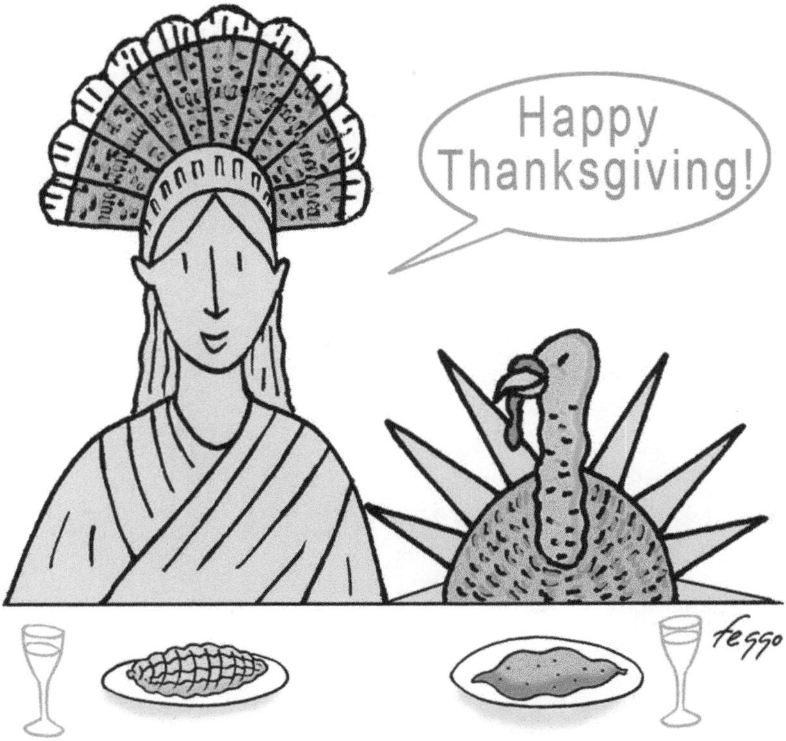
Happy Thanksgiving!
feggo

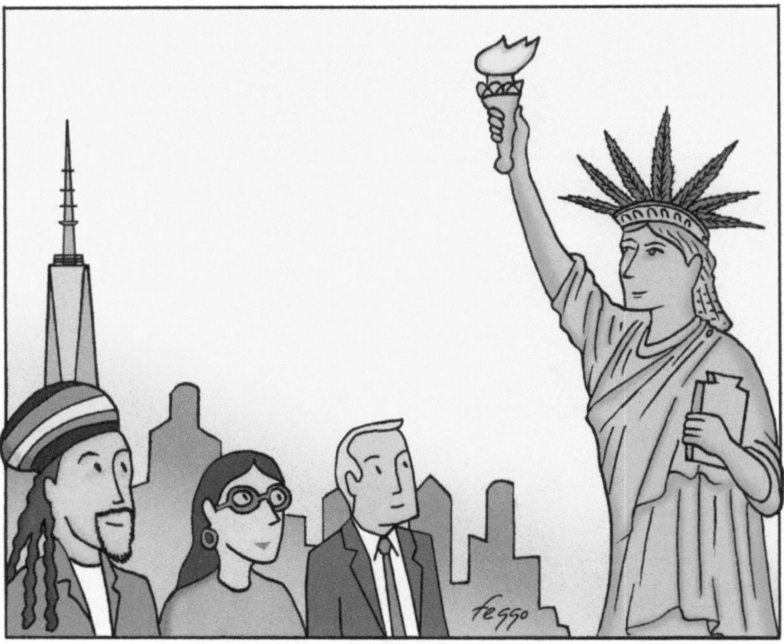
feggo

Exploitation

Many immigrants — including souvenir vendors — are virtually enslaved and forced to work under extreme conditions for little money, sometimes in order to pay back the steep smuggler's fees. In 1997 there was a case of 62 deaf and mute Mexican immigrants being forced to sell trinkets until finally the police intervened and apprehended their seven ringleaders. Instead of deportation, the exploited immigrants were later offered the opportunity to stay and get eventual residency. Some stayed, and one of them now works at Ellis Island near The Statue of Liberty, proving once again that the U.S. is a land of opportunity.

Explotación

Muchos inmigrantes — incluyendo vendedores de souvenirs — viven prácticamente esclavizados y son forzados a vender sus productos por poca remuneración y muchas veces, para pagar altas tarifas a los contrabandistas de personas. En 1997 hubo un caso en la ciudad de Nueva York donde 62 inmigrantes mexicanos sordomudos eran brutalmente explotados para vender baratijas, hasta que finalmente la policía intervino y apresó a los 7 jefes mafiosos. En lugar de deportarlos, las autoridades les ofrecieron permanecer en el país y obtener eventualmente residencia. Muchos aceptaron y uno de ellos trabaja ahora en Ellis Island, muy cerca de La Estatua de la Libertad, demostrando que este país es la tierra de las oportunidades.

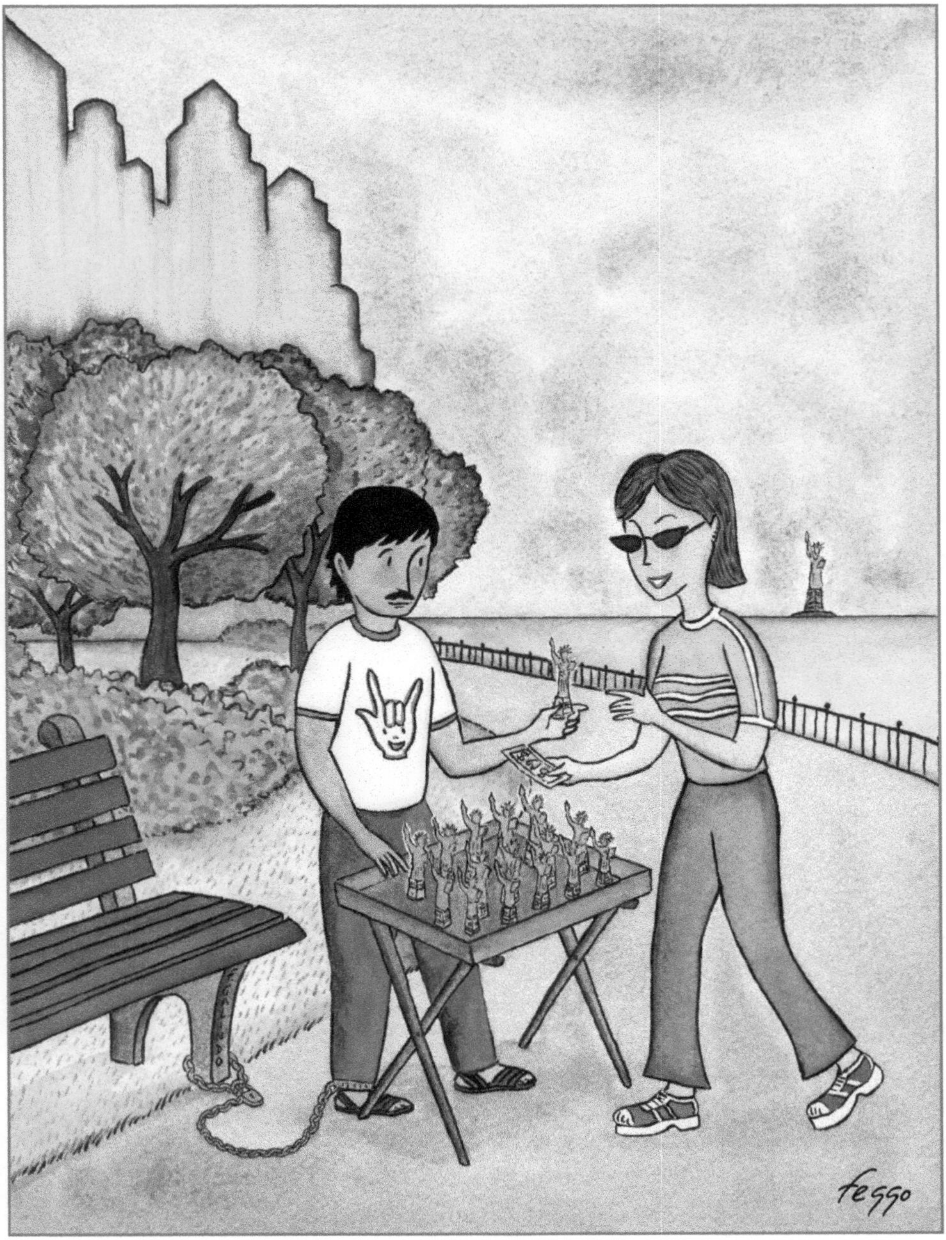
feggo

Passing the Torch

Illustration for the promotion of "The Good Ancestor Book" by British philosopher Roman Krznaric, published by Penguin Books, 2020.

Pasando La Antorcha

Ilustración para promover "El Libro del Buen Ancestro" del filósofo británico Roman Krznaric, Penguin Books, 2020.

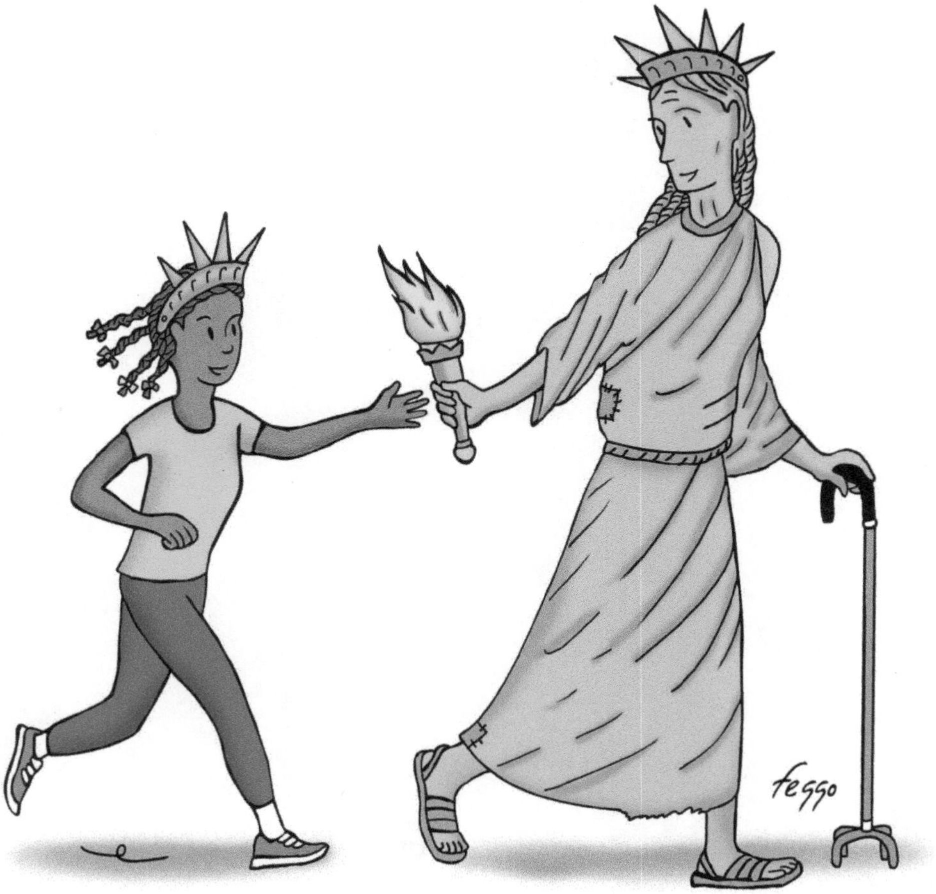
feggo

**Lady Liberty Visits the Whitney Museum's
Mexican Muralists Exhibition**

**La Dama Libertad Visita la Exhibición de los
Muralistas Mexicanos en el Museo Whitney**

Ella dice "Estos artistas mexicanos eran muy
buenos". El Tío Sam responde "¡Buenos agitadores
y promotores de ideas revolucionarias!

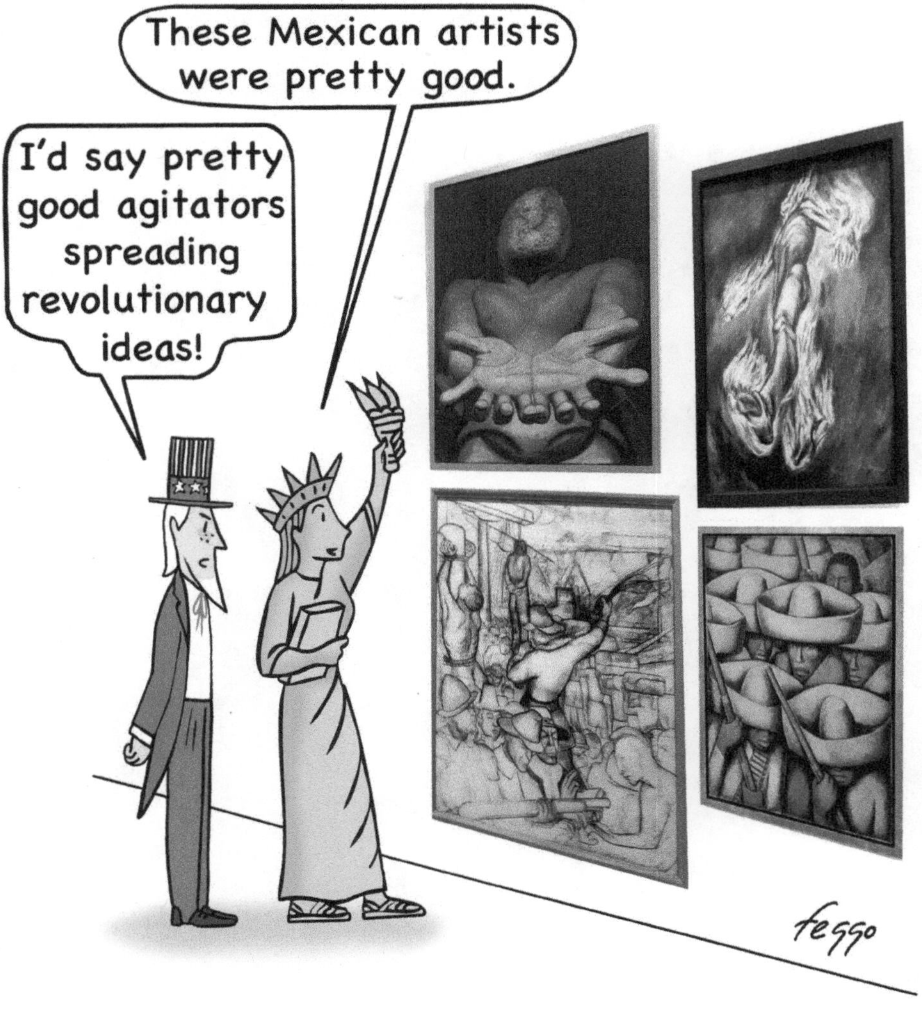
I'd say pretty good agitators spreading revolutionary ideas!
These Mexican artists were pretty good.
feggo

Altar to the Victims of COVID-19

Altar a las víctimas del COVID-19

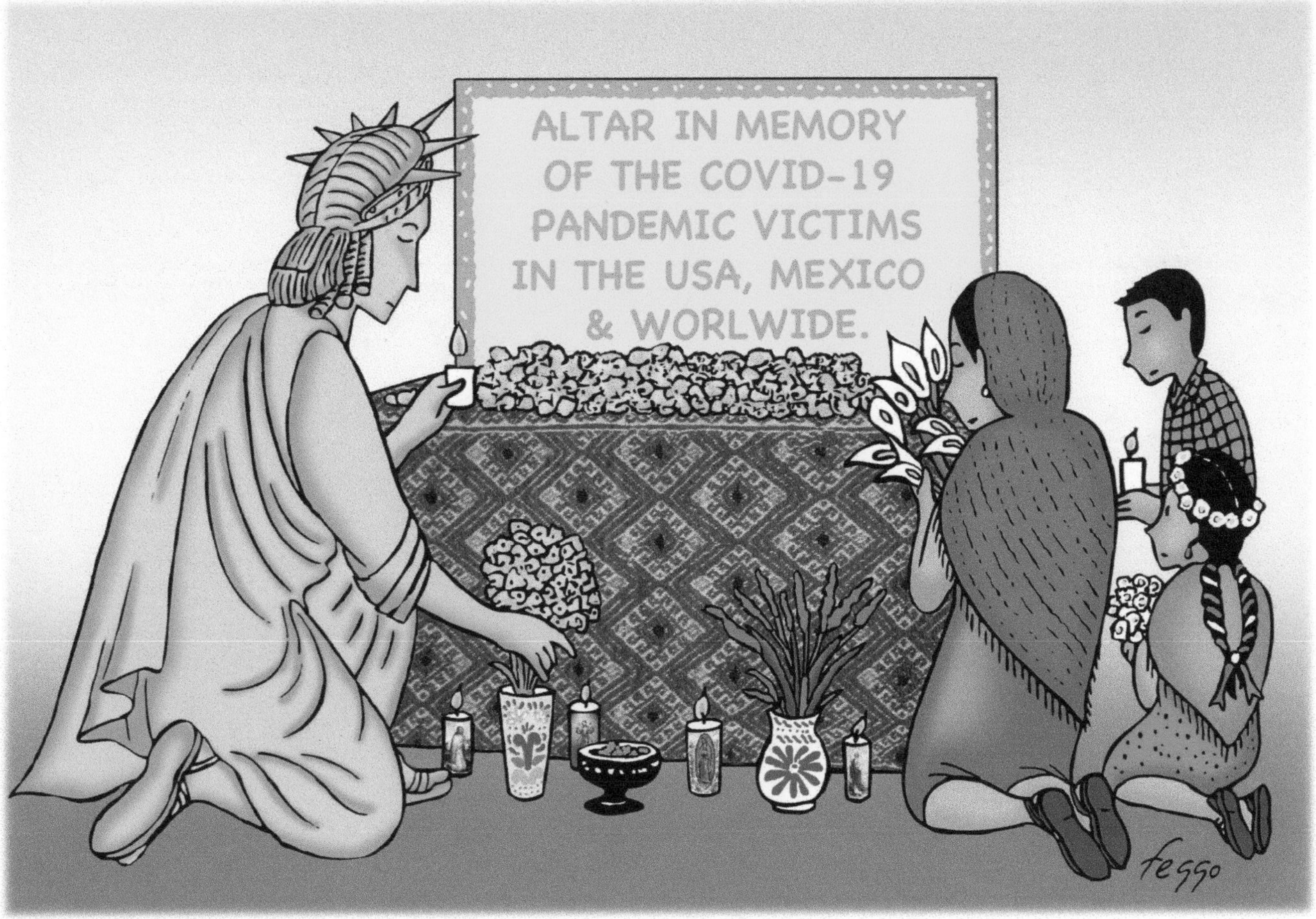
ALTAR IN MEMORY
OF THE COVID-19
PANDEMIC VICTIMS
IN THE USA, MEXICO
& WORLWIDE.
Feggo

4th of July

Part of the series "Used/Reused," artworks
utilizing discarded materials. Pastel and ink
drawing on a milk carton.

4 de Julio

De la serie "Usado/Reusado," obras utilizando
materiales de desecho. Tinta y pastel sobre
empaque de leche.

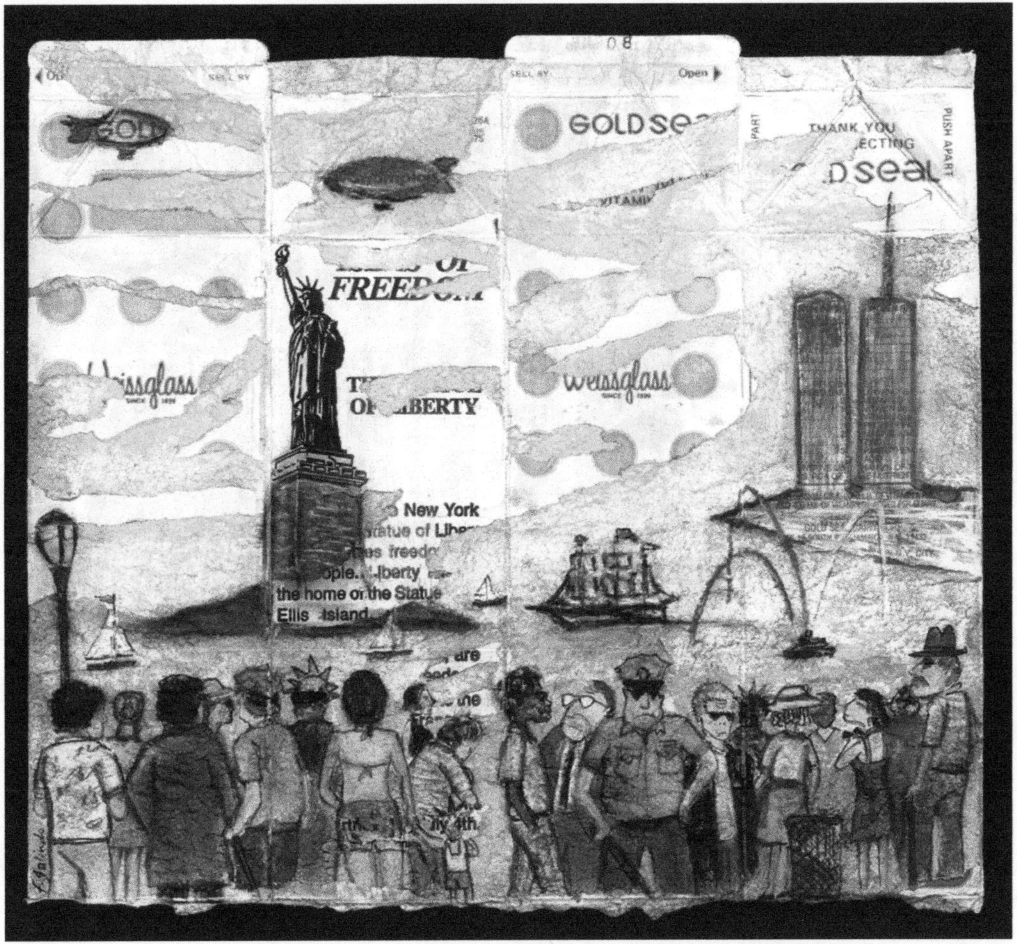

GOLD seal
THANK YOU
PUSH APART
FREEDOM
OF LIBERTY
New York
the home of the Statue
Ellis Island
Weissglass

Acknowledgements / Agradecimientos

Dedicated to all immigrants and to Andrea Arroyo, my partner
in our accidental immigration adventure.

Dedicado a todos los inmigrantes y a Andrea Arroyo,
mi compañera de aventuras en nuestra inmigración accidental.

Special thanks to the following persons and institutions:
Gracias especiales a las siguientes personas e instituciones:
Lower Manhattan Cultural Council, Martin Kozlowski, Julissa Reynoso, Frank di
Gregory, Debralee Santos, Sandra Fuentes-Berain, Armando Ponce, Barbara Winard,
Samantha Vuignier, Yaris Sedano, Juan Carlos Mercado, Melissa Esquivel, Santiago
Espinosa de los Monteros, Sarah Grass, Roman Krznaric, Cartoon Collections,
The U.S. Department of State.

These cartoons, illustrations, and artworks were published in:
Estos cartones, ilustraciones y arte fueron publicados en:
*The Nation, The Manhattan Times, amNY, Reason Magazine, Inxart.com, Political Telegram,
Unnaturalelection.com, The BMCC Journal, SVA's ContinuED,* Cartoonists & Writers
Syndicate, *The Spectator* (England), Revistas *Proceso, Emeequis* and
El Chamuco (Mexico), *Downtown Drowned* (Now What Media),
Nosotros Los Dreamers (Grijalbo.)

Works were also exhibited at: / Estos trabajos fueron exhibidos en:
The Morris-Jumel Mansion Museum, The Bronx Museum, The Interchurch Center,
Bronx Community College, Word-Up Bookstore, El Taller Latinoamericano,
Mark Miller Gallery, Azucarera Gallery, SVA Tribeca Gallery and
NYU Kimmel Galleries in New York City;
The Mexican Cultural Institute and the Center for Contemporary Political Art in
Washington, DC; Aydin Dogan Foundation, Istanbul, Turkey;
Porto CartoonFest, Portugal; US Embassy of Montevideo, Uruguay.

This book-catalog is a companion to "Taking Liberties," an exhibition of work on paper that was scheduled for the fall of 2020 at the art gallery of the CUNY Center for Worker Education in New York City, with the support of Lower Manhattan Cultural Council's Creative Engagement.

It had to be postponed due to the COVID-19 pandemic but it was offered online at my website *www.felipegalindo.com* from December 1, 2020 through April 30, 2021.

Este libro-catálogo es complemento de la exposición de dibujos "Tomarse Libertades," que estaba programada para el otoño de 2020 en la galería de arte del Centro para la Educación de los Trabajadores de CUNY en la ciudad de Nueva York, con apoyo del Lower Manhattan Cultural Council 's Creative Engagement, y que tuvo que posponerse debido a la pandemia de COVID-19.

Fue exhibida en línea en mi portal *www.felipegalindo.com* del 1o. de diciembre 2020 al 30 de abril de 2021.

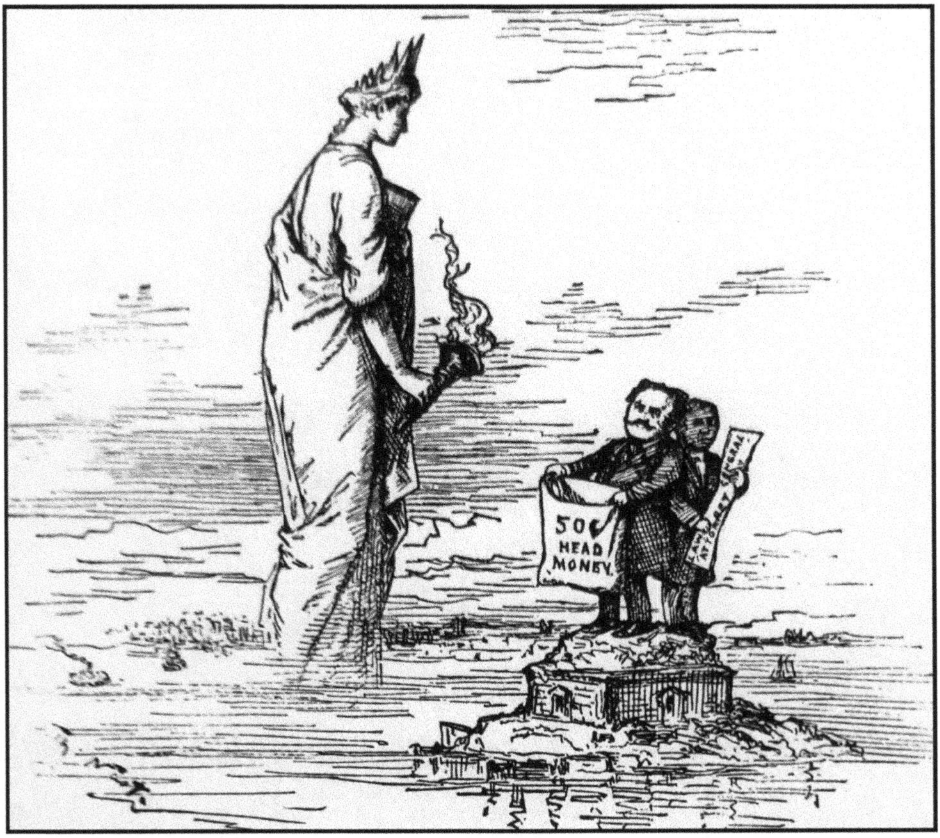
50¢
HEAD
MONEY.

In 1882 the U.S. government had a "head tax" policy of charging fifty cents to almost all foreigners entering the country at the time when Lady Liberty was being constructed. Here she is being asked to pay the "head tax" — also known as Poll Tax or Capitation, a tax levied as a fixed sum — before being permitted to mount her pedestal. (Artist unknown.)

En 1882, el gobierno de los Estados Unidos tenía una política de cobrar cincuenta centavos a casi todos los extranjeros que ingresaban al país en los años previos a que se inaugurara la Estatua de la Libertad. En este cartón político se le pide a ella que pague su "impuesto por cabeza" — también conocido como Poll Tax o Capitation, impuesto de suma fija — antes de que se le permita subir a su pedestal. (Dibujante desconocido.)

Other Books by Felipe Galindo Feggo

Manhatitlan: Mexican and American Cultures Intertwined (J. Pinto Books)

No Man Is a Desert Island (J. Pinto Books)

Cats Will Be Cats (Plume/Penguin)

George Washington: Back in New York City (Now What Media)

Other Now What Books

Silver Linings Plague Book

Gertrude et Alice

Trump Tweets Alt-American History

Talk to the Hair

**Flick and Flak:
More Poison Capsule Reviews**

The Golem's Voice

**Further Adventures:
Now What Anthology No. 1**

PK in the Terrarium

Downtown Drowned

The Da Vinci Cold

Go the F**k Back to Work!

Fairly Grim Tales

Love the Sinner, Hate the Cinema

Gertrude's Follies

INX Battle Lines: Three Decades of Political Illustration

CPSIA information can be obtained
at www.ICGtesting.com
Printed in the USA
BVHW062154140521
607271BV00008B/731